Smartphones as Locative Media

Jordan Frith

polity

First published in 2015 by Polity Press

Polity Press
65 Bridge Street
Cambridge CB2 1UR, UK

Polity Press
350 Main Street
Malden, MA 02148, USA

ISBN-13: 978-0-7456-8500-7
ISBN-13: 978-0-7456-8501-4(pb)

A catalogue record for this book is available from the British Library.

Typeset in 10.25 on 13 pt FF Scala by
Servis Filmsetting Ltd, Stockport, Cheshire
Printed and bound by Clays Ltd, St Ives plc

Library of Congress Cataloging-in-Publication Data

Frith, Jordan.
  Smartphones as locative media / Jordan Frith.
     pages cm. -- (Dms - digital media and society)
  Includes bibliographical references and index.
  ISBN 978-0-7456-8500-7 (hardback) -- ISBN 978-0-7456-8501-4 (paperback) 1.
Location-based services. 2. Mobile computing. 3. Smartphones. 4. Location-based
services--Social aspects. 5. Mobile computing--Social aspects. I. Title.
  TK5105.65.F78 2015
  004.167--dc23
                            2014030411

For further information on Polity, visit our website: politybooks.com

For Lindsay, I hope we're still going to Canada when we're 80

Contents

Acknowledgments

This book has a single author on the cover page, but it is the result of years of collaboration. Six years ago, Adriana de Souza e Silva – the first professor I had in my PhD program – approached me and asked if I wanted to work with her on a project. Before that moment, I had never heard the term "locative media," but luckily for me, Adriana got me interested in the topic. We ended up writing a couple articles and a book together, and I have been intrigued by the potential of locative media ever since. This project was born out of many of the ideas she and I worked on together through endless revisions, great conversations, and the kind of guidance any young scholar would be lucky to have.

And of course this book owes a great deal to other scholars as well. The field of mobile media studies, especially the subfield of locative media studies, is thriving but still small. That size meant that I got to know many of the people cited in this book, and people such as Jason Farman, Lee Humphreys, Christian Licoppe, Gerard Goggin, and Rowan Wilken could not have been kinder when I approached them at conferences or contacted them through email. Without their work and the insights of their many publications, this book would not be possible.

I also want to thank a variety of people who do not work directly in research on locative media. Carolyn Miller taught me how to approach the dynamic field of digital media, Steve Wiley convinced me to pay attention to culture and not exaggerate the effects of technology, Carole Blair introduced me to research on space and place and responded quickly to every email I ever wrote her, Jason Swarts introduced me to theories of technology that implicitly (and sometimes explicitly) shape my work, and

David Berube showed me how to approach a project in an organized fashion. Many other colleagues and friends – including Kathy Oswald, Jeff Swift, Jacob Dickerson, Rowan Wilken, Jason Kalin, and Jason Farman – also helped with the writing of this book by editing chapters and providing valuable feedback. The anonymous reviewers and especially Elen Griffiths – my editor at Polity – also gave me clear feedback that made the analysis in these pages so much stronger and clearer. I am thankful to all of you and know that this book is much stronger because of your help.

I also want to thank my family and friends. I never tell any of you what I'm working on, but you helped with this book more than you know. My mother was especially helpful because I could always call her up and talk about anything whenever I didn't feel like writing. And Lindsay, I couldn't have done this without you. You were there every step of the way, and you were the person I knew I could turn to whenever things got rough. Thank you for everything.

And finally, I want to thank Meagan, Daisy, and Hammond. They sat (mostly) patiently with me in my home office through all of my writing and went for walks with me whenever I got stuck. They're dogs, and I know they can't read, but just in case . . .

1

From Atoms to Bits and Back Again

Writing about emerging media presents a unique set of challenges. Whatever one writes will take long enough to complete and publish that many of the emerging media technologies analyzed will have changed. In few areas is that truer than in the study of mobile applications. In June, 2008, the Apple app store was still a month from being released; the Google app store did not exist. Slightly more than half a decade has now passed, and the mobile ecosystem has changed. Apple's app store has more than 1 million applications available for download, and the Android counterpart – the Google Play Store – now has over 1 million available applications that have been downloaded 50 billion times (Fiegerman, 2013).

Mobile applications are a key part of the move from basic feature phones to smartphones. Smartphones are mobile devices that allow people to place phone calls, send text messages, browse the Internet, use GPS and other forms of location awareness, and run third-party applications. Over half of all mobile phone users in at least 15 countries now own smartphones (Google, 2014), and the growth rates have been impressive. In the United States, 33 percent of the general population owned smartphones in 2011 compared to 56 percent just two years later (Smith, 2013); smartphone ownership rates in the UK nearly doubled over the same period (Ofcom, 2013). While many parts of the world have seen slower smartphone adoption, the International Telecommunication Union (ITU) points out that "In developing countries, the number of mobile broadband subscriptions more than doubled from 2011 to 2013" (ITU, 2013: 6). The increasing adoption of these miniature computers impacts the time and place of the Internet. Many people no longer only use the Internet in certain places at certain times. Instead, the mobile Internet becomes intertwined with people's everyday practices, operating in the background of many of their conversations and travels through physical space (Gordon and de Souza e Silva, 2011).

Smartphone usage does not represent a simple extension of older Internet practices. People do use their phones to accomplish many of the same tasks as they would with desktop and laptop computers. They check Facebook to see what their friends are doing; they go to Wikipedia to settle arguments; they browse their favorite websites. However, many smartphone applications add an important element to the way people interact with digital information: physical location. They do so because smartphones are examples of locative media. Locative media refers to any form of media – ranging from in-car GPS displays to RFID tags – that feature location awareness, which is a device's ability to be located in physical space and provide users with information about their surroundings. As covered in chapter 2, smartphones rely on a variety of techniques for location awareness, and these techniques are what enable applications like Google Maps and Yelp to know where a smartphone is on a map of physical space. Not all mobile applications take advantage of smartphones as locative media, but many do, and these mobile applications are called location-based services. They are the focus of this book.

Location-based services include everything from mapping services like Waze to popular social applications like Instagram that enable people to tag photos with location information. The applications are able to map different types of information because the pieces of digital information include latitude and longitude metadata, meaning they can be precisely placed on digital maps and positioned relationally to the location of the smartphone. Location is only one of many types of metadata included in the information with which users interact, but the argument throughout this book is that location data is an increasingly crucial piece of digital information (Gordon and de Souza e Silva,

2011). When people open up a smartphone application to provide them with information about their surroundings, they access digital information as an informational layer intertwined with the physical space they experience. Consequently, possibly the major social consequence of location-based services is that they not only impact the types of digital information people access, but they can also affect the way people navigate physical space and interact with those around them.

Smartphones as locative media show how physical places have begun to affect the mobile Internet and how the mobile Internet has begun to affect physical places. In some ways, the growth of location-based information seems like an obvious step in the maturation of the Internet. After all, why would people not use the information at their fingertips to learn more about the places they inhabit? However, to understand why smartphones as locative media represent a change in how the Internet is understood, it helps to examine how the Internet was originally conceived as "placeless." As the next section shows, many people argued that the Internet would make place less important. People would move their social lives online, spend most of their time in virtual communities, work from home, and congregate in and travel through physical space less and less (Kellerman, 2006). The implicit assumption, still present in expressions like "in real life" that oppose the offline to the online, is that the Internet represents a separate space from the physical world. The examples of location-based services detailed throughout this book show why the conceptual separation of the physical and digital into two separate spheres is untenable. Instead, the digital and physical are being merged in new ways, and this chapter concludes by explaining how the intertwining of the digital and physical is addressed in the rest of the book.

Communication media and the annihilation of space and place

Human beings can only cover a limited distance with their physical bodies. If people attempt to communicate a message with no outside assistance, the distance they can communicate is limited by how loud they can yell. People overcome this limitation through media technologies. Written language allowed people to transcribe messages that were transported to other places. The printing press allowed for the mass distribution of the same communication across physical space (Eisenstein, 1979). People even experimented with non-textual, non-verbal media to overcome physical distance. For example, African tribes developed an intricate language of "talking drum" beats that allowed towns to communicate across distance using sound (Gleick, 2011).

The growth of electronic media, first with the telegraph and then the radio and telephone, also enabled messages to overcome great distances. The telegraph was an important development in communication media and represented the first instance of people sharing textual messages across physical space without the need for physical travel (Carey, 1989). To send a letter or distribute a book, a human body had to physically transport the document. Telegraphs removed bodies from the equation, and the importance of that change did not go unnoticed by contemporary observers. For instance, an 1844 article in the *Baltimore Sun* about the completion of the Washington–Baltimore telegraph line claimed that "Time and space has been completely annihilated" (Rosen, 2012). This same feeling – that space was being annihilated through new communication media – was later echoed when people could transmit their voices through the telephone (Fischer, 1994; Marvin, 1988), broadcast messages into homes using the radio (Peters, 1999), and watch live events taking place on the other side of the world on television (Meyrowitz, 1985; Parks, 2005). These media, along with physical transportation technologies such as the railroad and airplanes (Schivelbusch, 1986), all contributed to the experience that physical space was being overcome. The far was brought near, the absent made present.

The Internet contributed to the same feeling of the annihilation of physical space, possibly to an even greater degree. With the development of the World Wide Web in the early 1990s, people were able to create chat rooms and Multi-User Domains to build relationships with distant others (Baym, 2010), companies built global networks of information flows that lessened the importance of national borders (Castells, 2000), and many scholars and popular sources argued that the Web would lessen the importance of physical space (Gordon and de Souza e Silva, 2011). This sentiment can be seen in a famous 1994 MCI commercial about the Internet. The commercial featured a 12-year-old Anna Paquin describing the "Information Super Highway" as a road that will connect all points on the globe. The most famous statement from the commercial is when Paquin says this road "will not go from here to there. There will be no more there. We will all only be here" ("No More There," 1994). Few quotes better encapsulate the belief that distinct places would be made meaningless by the new communication technology of the Internet. The Internet would allow people to be everywhere all at once, overcoming distance and lessening the importance of being in any one place at a given time.

Even the dominant earlier metaphor of the Internet – cyberspace – showed how people viewed the online world as separate from physical spaces, so separate that it needed its own spatial metaphor to differentiate it from other parts of daily life. And some cultural critics went so far as to argue that cyberspaces would begin to replace the importance of physical spaces. One of the most famous thinkers to do so was Nicholas Negroponte (1995), the founder of the MIT Media Lab. Negroponte's predictions opposed the world of atoms (the physical) to the world of bits (the digital). He argued that the future lay in bits not atoms, whether in the forms of digital spaces in which to socialize or digital spaces in which to trade (Morgan, 2004). As Negroponte claimed,

> As we interconnect ourselves, many of the values of the nation-state will give way to those of both larger and smaller electronic communities. We will socialize in digital neighborhoods in which physical space will be irrelevant and time will play a different role. (Negroponte, 1995: 6)

Negroponte predicted that people would turn away from physical space to live their lives online.[1] He was not alone in this line of thought. Futurists such as Hans Moravec (1990) imagined worlds in which people download their consciousness into wired mainframes. Philosopher Paul Virilio (1997) expressed fear that the age of instant access would lead to a future in which people would not even care about the physical world enough to meet up to have sex. People were supposedly heading toward a future in which the life of the body was replaced by life on a screen. As is fairly obvious, these predictions of the world of atoms being overcome by the world of bits never fully played out in reality.

Early Internet research did suggest that people who spent more time online tended to interact less offline (Kraut et al., 1998). However, these findings changed as more people went online and more scholars began studying the interactions between digital and physical sociability (Kraut et al., 2002). Sociologists Lee Rainie and Barry Wellman's (2012) book *Networked: The New Social Operating System* is an excellent synthesis of statistical research that shows people who spend more time communicating online also tend to spend more time communicating with people offline in physical space. Research has also shown that, in contrast to predictions that people would turn to the Internet as a substitution for physical travel, people who use the Internet frequently do not travel significantly less (Kellerman, 2006). Rather than replacing the need for physical social interaction and mobility, the Internet has instead been enfolded into people's everyday lives (Baym, 2010), and the online and offline "intersect with one another in a complex fashion" (Morgan, 2004: 5). People still travel to work, meet with friends, and walk city streets. They just now often do so in a way that intertwines the world of atoms with the world of bits.

While it is possible to look at oppositions of the digital and physical as outdated, strands of that thought survive today. People still use the phrase "in real life" (IRL) to compare interactions in the physical world to something that happens online, and best-sellers such as Sherry Turkle's (2010) *Alone Together* still argue that online life is distracting people from the physical world. The implication is that individuals have a physical life (real life) and an online life (unreal life?). "In real life" implies that what happens online is somehow less important, despite the relationships people build online and the online resources they use to accomplish a variety of offline tasks (Baym, 2010). The separation becomes even more tenuous when analyzing the uses of smartphones as locative media. Offline interactions are increasingly permeated by digital data, particularly through the growth of location-based services that provide people with information about their surrounding spaces.

The place of locative media

The number of mobile applications has increased rapidly over the last half decade, with more than a million applications available on Android phones and iPhones. Many of the most popular applications are location-based services. A national survey in the United States found that 74 percent of adult smartphone users use their phone to get information about their surrounding space (Zickuhr, 2013), and a national survey in the UK found that 69 percent of smartphone users access maps through their device (Ofcom, 2013). That 69 percent likely underrepresents the number of people who use location-based services because these applications cover far more than just mapping services. Review sites like Yelp use location to provide people with information; Facebook allows people to tag their posts with location information; Instagram includes location information in the photos people share.

These examples all show why it is not analytically useful to keep trying to separate the physical and the digital. Instead, location-based services merge the two into what communication scholar Adriana de Souza e Silva (2006) calls a "hybrid space" – a key concept that forms part of the theoretical framework in the following chapters. Hybrid spaces are formed through a combination of three elements: social interaction, digital information, and physical space. The digital information people access in hybrid spaces is not exterior to the place; it becomes a part of that place for the user, just as a street sign or other physical informational becomes a part of a place. Hybrid space is a valuable conceptual tool because it refuses the urge to separate location-based digital information from the physical place it describes.[2] Instead, the digital plays a role in shaping how people "read" physical places (de Souza e Silva and Frith, 2012). If people use their smartphones to pull up a list of nearby restaurants on the mobile application Yelp, other people's reviews can impact how they read their surroundings and make choices about a place. If people report an accident on the highway using the mobile application Waze, they might encourage others to make an alternative mobility choice because of the merging of the digital and physical in the hybrid space. As sociologist Michael Hardey (2007) argued, digital location information "is providing new ways of seeing, experiencing and understanding the city" (p. 867).

These new ways of seeing and experiencing the city show why smartphones as locative media require an understanding of more than how people interact with their mobile screens; analyses need to examine how these interactions impact people's experience of their surrounding space. The focus on the relationship between locative media and place is the major thread tying the following chapters together, and unlike some media studies approaches, this book draws from spatial thinkers to discuss how the growth of hybrid spaces may impact society. Chapter 2 introduces key concepts to understand the social impacts of locative media and begins by focusing on the importance of place in people's social worlds before moving on to the mobilities turn, which focuses on the crucial role movement plays in people's lives. After all, mobile media, ranging from the newspaper to the smartphone, are tools people use to exert control over their experience of physical movement (de Souza e Silva and Frith, 2012). And as shown in chapter 2, locative media represent a shift in the already complicated relationship between mobile media and place.

After establishing a conceptual framework in chapter 2, chapter 3 provides background on how location-based services work. The chapter explains location awareness by detailing GPS, Wi-Fi-enabled location, and cellular triangulation before moving on to an account of mobile "generations" to show how mobile telephony arrived at the 3G and 4G mobile connections so crucial to the growth of location-based services. The chapter concludes by discussing the two most popular smartphone operating systems – Android and iOS – and explaining how the growth of app stores has changed the mobile media landscape.

Chapters 4–6 analyze three types of location-based services: navigation applications, social networking applications, and applications that allow people to contribute and access geotagged information. Chapter 6 also mentions mobile gaming, though this book does not devote a chapter to mobile gaming because so much excellent research already exists on the topic (cf. Hjorth, 2011). Each of these chapters examines specific location-based services, but the focus is more on user practices and how location information impacts people's experiences than on the design of any specific application. As digital media researcher Nancy Baym (2010) wrote,

> Trying to list specific types of digital media is frustrating at best. Between this writing and your reading there are bound to be new developments, and things popular as I write will drop from vogue. *Let this be a reminder to us of the importance of remaining focused on specific capabilities and consequences rather than the media themselves.* (p. 13; italic emphasis added)

Baym's advice applies to the study of location-based services. Some of the mobile applications discussed in this book might not exist by the time the book is published; other applications may be updated and look significantly different than they do now. For this reason, chapters 4–6 analyze the consequences and capabilities of location-based services rather than specific applications as a way to ensure the analysis in this book will remain useful regardless of the ways in which the mobile applications examined change.

The focus on practices rather than individual applications shifts in chapter 7, which moves away from user practices to instead discuss the location-based service Foursquare. The chapter uses Foursquare as a case study to explain how market forces can shape contemporary location-based services because Foursquare is an interesting example that split its features into two separate applications (Foursquare and Swarm) in part to address a shift in the developers' overall goals. Some of the applications analyzed in chapters 4–6 are relatively new startups, and they must seek out funding sources and ways to monetize their service. By looking at how one specific application has managed the business side of mobile development, chapter 7 shows that these applications do not develop in a vacuum. They collect data and offer services with the goal of eventually becoming viable businesses. The discussion of location information as commercial data continues in chapter 8, which analyzes privacy issues that accompany the sharing of location information with other individuals, as well as the ways in which governments and law enforcement use location data.

The book ends with an eye to the future. Chapters 2–8 focus mostly on the industrialized world, both because of my research experience and because smartphones have not been as widely adopted in the global South; however, as discussed in the concluding chapter, that will likely change in the near future as cheaper smartphones hit the market and adoption increases in the developing world. The final chapter also raises questions about how the growth of hybrid spaces and the reliance on location-based services may lead to new forms of inequality, and the book concludes by discussing how the potential future of "The Internet of Things" may affect the ways people use smartphones as locative media.

The following chapters cover a variety of topics, but the central thread tying them together is the argument that smartphones as locative media have begun to shift how people experience physical place. Locative media show how online data now shapes offline experiences. As discussed above, the Internet was originally conceived of as placeless, but location-based services show that digital information is increasingly organized around physical locations. That shift is a major one, and it has contributed to a partial change in how spaces are produced and understood through digital information accessed through smartphone screens. People can never be sure what the future holds for emerging media, but they can attempt to capture the present moment in a way that will help them understand what comes next. The following chapters focus on theory and user practices that will help in analyzing the contemporary moment of locative media and the future impacts as location information further shapes interactions with both digital information and physical space.

2

Mobilities and the Spatial Turn

This chapter might be read as part of a printed book. It might be read on an eReader, on a tablet computer, or on a mobile phone. Regardless of how the chapter is accessed, the person reading it is *in place*. The place might be a dorm room or a library, an apartment or a coffee shop. The reader might be able to glance around the room and remember things that happened there, or she might have no particular attachment to the place at all. Either way, she is still occupying a physical place reading this text. This chapter is about that place and so many others.

"Place" is a term used all the time. People ask friends if they want to come over to their place. Family members talk about the places they visited over the summer. If two friends feel homesick right now or wish they were somewhere else, they long for one place over another. Place structures much of individuals' thought and memory, yet despite how commonly people use the term, "place is clearly a complicated concept" (Cresswell, 2004: 50). But it is a concept that remains centrally important to the world and raises questions about how the experience of place changes with the introduction of emerging media. As a thought experiment on why place has such a complex relationship to media usage, return to the first paragraph. As this chapter is read, the reader is physically in place somewhere. However, imagine for a second that rather than reading this academic book, the reader is fully engrossed in the narrative of her favorite novel. That novel likely has a physical setting, for example the nineteenth-century English countryside of Jane Austen or George R. R. Martin's Westeroos. Those are both places even though they are not physical places like a dorm room or a coffee shop. The "imagined places" of novels raise an important question for media studies scholars (Jansson and Falkheimer, 2006), particularly those that study mobile technologies: are people still "in place" in a dorm room or library if they are also engrossed in the imagined place of the novel? Some variation of that question has shaped much of the analysis of mobile media, ranging from the Walkman to the mobile phone (de Souza e Silva and Frith, 2012). When people call someone or engage with their mobile phone screen, are they still fully present in the physical place they move through? How are the answers to these questions impacted by locative media?

To best address these questions, it is important to explore how people understand place. To do so, this chapter first discusses the "spatial turn" and the "mobilities turn" in the humanities and social sciences, which are two related theoretical movements that shed light on the prominent position of place in the social world. The chapter then analyzes how people use older forms of mobile media, such as the book, the Walkman, and the mobile phone, to exert some control over their experience of movement, and it concludes by explaining how locative media shift the relationship between mobile media and place.

The importance of the space and place

Social theory is filled with binaries people use to understand the social world. Academic thought has absence/presence, virtual/ physical, and private/public to name a few. One of the dominant binaries throughout much social theory of the nineteenth and twentieth centuries was space and time. Time was often seen as the more important of the two (Massey, 2005). Time was viewed as dynamic and progressive and was used to mark the "stages" or "eras" of human development, seen notably in Marshall McLuhan's media eras or Karl Marx's stages of history. Space and place, on the other hand, have often been viewed "as a location on a surface where things 'just happen' rather than the more holistic view of places as the geographical context for the mediation of physical, social and economic processes" (Agnew,

2011: 317). As geographers John Agnew and James Duncan (1989) claimed, "the concept of place has been marginalized within the discourse of modern social science and history" (p. 2).

Space and place began to see a resurgence in academic thought in the 1970s and 1980s with the "spatial turn" in the humanities and social sciences. Human geographers Yi Fu Tuan (1977) and Edward Relph (1976) developed influential work that focused on how people experience place. Philosophers Michel de Certeau (1988) and Henri Lefebvre (1991) analyzed how spaces are socially produced and how that production shapes the lived experience of individuals. Lefebvre and de Certeau also dealt explicitly with the role space and place play in producing and reproducing power structures, a focus adopted by important cultural geographers such as David Harvey (1991), Doreen Massey (1994), and Edward Soja (1996). These thinkers all raised different questions about space and place, and they came from different disciplinary backgrounds. However, what united the work of the major thinkers mentioned above was an agreement that space and place play a key role in how people experience the world.

The effects of the spatial turn in cultural theory are still being felt today as more social scientific and humanistic disciplines adopt the work of major spatial thinkers. The effect has already been felt in media studies research, which was fairly quick to recognize the ways in which emerging media can affect people's sense of place. One of the earliest, most influential examples was communication scholar Joshua Meyrowitz's (1985) book *No Sense of Place*, which examined how television exposed people to new places and altered impressions of their local environment. Media theorists Nick Couldry and Anne McCarthy's (2004) edited collection *MediaSpace* also provided a detailed account of how spatial configurations relate to media consumption. At the center of this research and the mobile media research examined later is the question of how people's sense of place is impacted as they adopt new media. However, to best analyze the spatial impacts of mobile media, it helps to examine the different ways place has been conceptualized and outline the definition drawn from throughout the rest of this book.

Conceptualizing place

"Place" is the kind of indeterminate, subjective term that frustrates attempts at simple definition. Think of how people use the word in terms of scale. A home is often thought of as a place ("want to come over to my place?"). Even a room in a home can be a place distinct from other rooms. But a neighborhood can also be a place, and on a larger scale, so can cities and nations. The complication of scale raises the question of what people mean when they talk about place. In many ways, the answer is subjective. Places are where individuals make them. Tuan (1977) describes this idea in his opposition of the terms "space" and "place": "what begins as an undifferentiated space becomes place as we get to know it better and endow it with value" (p. 6). In Tuan's terms, space and place are a necessary binary. Space is "that which allows movement" and "place is pause; each pause in movement makes it possible for location to be transformed into place" (p. 6).

Tuan's opposition of space and place arises frequently.[1] For example, Relph (1976) also viewed space as the abstract multitude from which individuals carve out a sense of place. Other scholars, such as philosopher Edward Casey (1996) and computer scientists Steve Harrison and Paul Dourish (1996),[2] opposed space – seen as the abstraction of a geometrically measured product of science – to place as the lived experience. What is key to all these conceptualizations is that place becomes more than a site upon which people act. Place instead plays a role in shaping action and identity. As Casey (1996) wrote, "To live is to live locally, and to know is first of all to know the place one is in" (p. 18).

The idea of living locally directly relates to the media studies and the mobilities research I discuss later. One of the fears expressed about communication media and globalization in general is that they potentially damage the authenticity of individual places. These arguments often focus on how people's increased movement and their ability to use communication technologies to communicate with distant others contribute to homogenization and placelessness (Relph, 1976). An example of this argument can be found in the work of anthropologist Marc Augé (1995), who argued that human lives are increasingly filled with "non-places" that lose their meaning and distinction from other places. Augé defined non-places as "spaces of circulation (freeways, airways), consumption (department stores, supermarket), and communication (telephones, faces, television, cable networks)" (p. 110). No doubt, if Augé had been writing five years later, the Internet likely would have been one of his prime non-places.

Augé's concept of non-places has been influential but has been criticized for ignoring the place-making tendencies of humans (Merriman, 2004). I grew up in Virginia in the suburbs of Washington, DC. These suburbs featured the types of homogenization Augé and others who write about "placeless-ness" discuss (Relph, 1976). The movie theater closest to my house is one of four movie theaters within a 5 mile radius. All four are located in shopping centers that might seem the same to an outsider. But I remember one as the place I got my first job as a 15-year-old. I can still tell stories about that job. That movie theater and those shopping centers may seem interchangeable, but going back to Tuan, Casey, and others, humans construct a sense of place regardless. An airport that might be a non-place for one person might be the place another met his wife.

The case of the airport also raises interesting questions about place and mobility. Mobility can refer to many things, including people's ability to move through physical space (physical mobil-ity) or the ability to substitute physical travel with phone calls or Internet searches (virtual mobility) (Kellerman, 2006). These forms of mobility are part of what Augé and Relph argue con-tribute to the increasing homogenization of place. However, the idea that places can be "authentic" or that movement (whether virtual or physical) harms a sense of place has been questioned by other scholars, including geographer Doreen Massey (1994).

Massey argued that geographers must adopt a "progressive sense of place" that recognizes that communication media and transportation technologies can actually *increase* one's sense of place because the understanding of the local is always formed relationally ("my town is different from that town because ..."). In her conceptualization of place that I adopt throughout this book, she pointed out that places are not "local" in the sense they can be viewed as fixed, bounded, and authentic. Instead, places are always the sites of flows. What makes a place distinct is the types of information, people, and goods that flow through it, and in a later work, Massey (2005) described place as a specific set of trajectories coming into contact. Her view of place as the process, rather than result, of various flows opens up the understanding of place. Places are not self-contained; they are not static. Instead, "what gives a place its specificity is not some long internalized history but the fact that it is constructed out of a particular constellation of social relations, meeting and weaving together at a particular locus" (Massey, 1994: 154).

Understanding place as open rather than closed, as dynamic rather than static, allows for the analysis of how the social construction of place happens from both the inside and outside. Notably, a "progressive sense of place" also recognizes the importance of movement, which is key to understanding the ways in which people use mobile media to shape their experience of place.

Movement and openness

The late 1990s and 2000s saw a further "turn" in academic thought called "the mobilities turn." The mobilities turn builds on the spatial turn and focuses on movement of all types, whether physical movement, virtual movement, material movement, or even imaginary movement (Sheller and Urry, 2006). The focus on mobility is important because even as spatial analysis has increased, "travel has been for the social sciences seen as a black box, a neutral set of technologies and processes" (Sheller and Urry, 2006: 208). In other words, approaches to space and place often view movement as "dead time" spent going from one place to another (Green, 2002; Lyons and Urry, 2005). In traditional analyses, it was the destination that mattered, not the journey. Mobilities researchers, on the other hand, still value the importance of fixed destinations, but they argue that experiences of place cannot be divorced from the flows of both people and things: "Places are thus not so much fixed but are implicated within complex networks by which 'hosts, guests, buildings, objects and machines' are contingently brought together to produce certain performances in certain places at certain times" (Hannam, Sheller, and Urry, 2006: 13).

Mobilities researchers' establishment of a "movement-driven social science" (Urry, 2007: 18) is, in part, an attempt to rethink the concept of place by positioning place as the result of flows of various kinds. The focus on movement raises questions about how places are socially produced: how are places positioned in the various networks of people, ideas, and material that flow in the global economy (Sheller, 2010)? Who is allowed to move freely and who has their mobility either restricted or forced (Cresswell, 2010)? How do people use mobile technologies to influence their experience of movement (de Souza e Silva and Frith, 2010b; Wilken, 2010)? The answers to these questions and many others are what make up the performative identity of place, which contrasts with some influential concepts of place discussed in the previous section. Tuan defined space as movement and place as pause. Augé viewed sites of transit as the "non-places" of contemporary life. The mobilities turn, in contrast, sees place as the result of flows, not pause. Equally importantly, sites of transit and movement are not separate from the construction of place. Without understanding how people experience movement, scholars cannot understand how a place's identity is performed (Jensen, 2009).

One of the valuable contributions of the mobilities turn has been the recognition of the role technologies play in the experience of mobility and the construction of place. Much of this research has focused on transportation technologies. For instance, Wolfgang Schivelbusch's (1986) work on train travel showed how the railway compressed space and time by reducing travel time between cities. Other mobilities research focused on how people use mobile technologies to mediate their experience of movement (Frith, 2012b; Wilken, 2010). The next section examines earlier forms of mobile media from a mobilities perspective to show the complex relationship between mobile media use and place.

Mobile media and spatial experience[3]

Computer scientist Alan Kay half-jokingly claimed that "technology is anything that was invented after you were born" (quote in Kelly, 2005: n.p.). Kay's joke obviously does not work as a rigorous definition of technology, but in many ways the definition applies to many people's understanding of mobile media. When I ask my students what they think of when I use the term "mobile media," almost no one ever mentions older media like the paperback novel. However, books are an important mobile media form people used to control their experience of movement and place.

The paperback book became popular in the mid-nineteenth century and is still popular today. To some degree, paperback books' popularity and availability were made possible by new developments in printing technologies (Manguel, 1997). However, their rapid growth in popularity was also a result of changing mobility practices (de Souza e Silva and Frith, 2012). The mid-nineteenth century was the period in which railway travel began to take off in the UK. Miles of tracks were built, and people who rode the railway were confronted with a new social situation: they were forced to travel with strangers for extended periods of time in contrast to the more private setting of the eighteenth-century coach (de Souza e Silva and Frith, 2012; Manguel, 1997; Schivelbusch, 1986). To negotiate this new form of mobility, people turned to paperback novels as a technology that allowed them to exert a certain sense of control over their experience of the setting and mediate their experience of place. They could use the book or the newspaper to engage with a text rather than the strangers in their shared compartment, and "Our current assumption that 'travel' means 'reading' arrived only with the railways" (Flanders, 2006: n.p).

People still use books to mediate their experience of mobility, but they are just as likely to have headphones in their ears as they are to have their head in a book, a tendency that began in 1977 when Sony released the original Walkman. The Walkman was a cultural sensation, and as Adriana de Souza e Silva and I (2012) argued, much of the marketing of the Walkman focused on a combination of mobility and privacy. People were able to listen to music while mobile and exert control over the private auditory environment with which they interacted (du Gay, Hall, Janes, Mackay, and Negus, 1997). Later forms of mobile media, most notably the iPod, gave people even more control over their experience of movement because they could carry their "auditory identity in the palm of [their] hand" (Bull, 2006: 145). They could basically pick a song to match their mood, and that song would become a soundtrack to their movement through physical space.

Here is where the earlier theories of place and mobility become so crucial to understanding how people use these mobile technologies. Place, using a common definition, is a meaningful location, and critics have argued that people use mobile media to make place less meaningful by engaging in the mediated space of the song or the narrative of a novel rather than their physical surroundings (Bloom, 1988; Gergen, 2002). One example of this criticism is Du Gay and colleagues' (1997) book about the Sony Walkman, which examined how the Walkman complicated the division between private and public because people turned to the private experience of headphones rather than the public spaces they moved through. Sociologist Michael Bull (2000, 2007), in his extensive ethnographic work with Walkman and iPod users, made similar arguments. His work revealed that people construct "mobile media sound bubbles" that allow them to shield themselves from the actual auditory experience of a place: "It appears that as consumers become immersed in their mobile media sound bubbles, so those spaces habitually passed through in daily life increasingly lose significance and turn progressively into the 'nonspaces' of daily life that users try, through those self-same technologies, to transcend" (Bull, 2004: 189).

The mobile phone has been analyzed in much the same way as these other forms of mobile media. Analyses of the mobile phone frequently featured discussions of how mobile voice calls distracted people from their experience of place. In particular, mobile phone research included multiple examinations of how mobile phones allowed people to bring private relationships into public space (De Gournay, 2002; Hoflich, 2005), and psychologist Kenneth Gergen (2002) claimed that people who talk on their mobile phones are not fully inhabiting that physical place. Instead, he argued that mobile phone users enact a form of "absent presence." They may be physically present in a place, but they are rendered absent because they are more engaged in their remote conversation than their physical surroundings. Gergen's view that mobile phones damaged experience of place has been echoed in many popular press accounts that view mobile phones as lessening people's connection to the places they move through (Quenida, 2013). These criticisms of mobile telephony are basically criticisms of the ways in which people use mobile media to control their experiences of mobility.

To some degree, some of these criticisms of mobile media are overstated. Research shows that people who use mobile media still find ways to engage with place (Gordon and de Souza e Silva, 2011; Humphreys, 2005; Ling, 2004). People may seem distracted while talking on mobile phones or walking around with headphones in their ears, but that does not mean they experience a form of placelessness (de Souza e Silva and Frith, 2012). Instead, they enact a different form of mobility, mediating their movement through mobile media and altering their sense of place. Returning to Massey, there is no "authentic" sense of place to be polluted by the use of mobile media; instead, the place changes as the constellations of people and technologies found in one physical location changes. However, while the mobile phone, the book, and mobile auditory media do not lead to true placelessness, they do contribute to a more isolated experience of place than the forms of locative media examined in the rest of this book. The final section of this chapter discusses how locative media complicate traditional understandings of the interaction between mobile media and place.

What changes with locative media

Reading, listening to music, and talking on a mobile phone are three different activities. All three activities, however, have at least one significant thing in common: they introduce an informational layer to one's experience of place that is exterior to that place (de Souza e Silva and Frith, 2012). Whether it is the narrative of a novel, a favorite song, or a phone conversation with a friend, these are all forms of mediation that are not place-dependent. People can listen to the same song or have the same mobile phone conversation regardless of their physical location. In a sense, the fact that this layer of mediation feels so separate, so private, is key to why mobile media have often been criticized as detracting from a sense of place.

Locative media work on a different principle. Unlike the iPod or a text message to a friend, the information people access when they use locative media is *about* the places they inhabit. The location-based digital information is tied closely to that place, not an exterior informational layer introduced through the text of a book or a song blared through headphones. Compare two possible experiences with a mobile phone. The first experience involves walking down a street while talking to a friend on the phone. The phone user contacts a distant person rather than engaging with anyone nearby or paying close attention to her surroundings. The second experience involves the person standing on that same street and using her phone to look at a mapping application. She clicks through the application and pulls up the "restaurant" category to see a map of nearby places. She finds a list of places, reads what other people wrote about the places, and then maps a route from her location to the restaurant she chose. She is able to engage in these two activities with her smartphone, just like she can listen to music or read an eBook on her smartphone. But using a location-based service suggests a different relationship between her mobile device and her surrounding space. The information she receives depends on her physical location, meaning she would receive a different set of spatially encoded information if she stood on a different street in a different city (de Souza e Silva and Sutko, 2011). The same is not true for the mobile phone call or music played through her headphones.

Here is where the concept of hybrid space examined in the previous chapter is useful for understanding the social impacts of smartphones as locative media. Hybrid space conceptualizes what happens as the Internet leaves the desktop and moves out into the physical world. Importantly, however, hybrid spaces are not just places affected by the location-based information of the mobile Internet; hybrid spaces are also spaces that show how physical place shapes the meaning of the mobile Internet. In a hybrid space, the physical location determines the information one receives, just as the location-based information influences how people move through and make decisions about their physical space. The smartphone screen then becomes a way for people to mediate their experience of space and movement by accessing spatial information.

The ways in which spatial information converges and is organized around different locations also show why Massey's progressive sense of place can be such a useful conceptual tool for understanding locative media because it shows how place is dynamic and always changing. Seeing a friend share a location on Facebook or Instagram can make a place seem more appealing. Bad reviews on an application like Yelp or Socialight can make a place seem less desirable. An alternative route on a mapping application may encourage someone to make a different mobility choice. The person's experience of place may change as new types of location-based information become embedded in nearby locations, meaning that the place as a collection of specific trajectories shifts as new, more durable trajectories make their mark on a place through the digital traces they leave behind. The shifting of trajectories, the change in the informational layers composing contemporary places, is the major reason why locative media are important from a social perspective. Place is not static; it does not have a fixed meaning that cannot change. Instead, place is dynamic and open to new flows of information, so people's sense of place can be impacted as they adopt new mobile applications and find new ways to use locative media to negotiate experiences of physical and virtual mobility. Ultimately, as researchers Paul Dourish and Genevieve Bell (2011) argue, locative media "become a new lens through which the spatialities of urban space can be viewed" (p. 120). As the spatial turn suggests, how people see and experience place matters, and that experience can alter as people enfold new forms of mobile media into their everyday lives.

Conclusion

For much of the twentieth century, space and place were viewed by philosophers and other scholars as less important than time (Massey, 2005). Time was where the action happened; time was how people marked progress and the dynamic changes of history. Space and place, on the other hand, were often viewed as static sites where time passed. That began to change with the spatial turn in the humanities and social sciences. The spatial turn refocused attention on the importance of space and place. Human geographers such as Yi Fu Tuan (1977) and Edward Relph (1976) began to think deeply about how people understand place, and other scholars, such as Henri Lefebvre (1991) and David Harvey (1991), began to analyze the vital role space and place play in the social world.

While the spatial turn brought place to the forefront of some lines of thought, thinkers still tended to view place as rather static. Tuan viewed place as pause; Relph opposed "authentic" places to placelessness, criticizing media and mobility as damaging the importance of place. In response, scholars began examining the crucial role mobility plays in the social construction of place. One of the most influential scholars to do so was geographer Doreen Massey (1994). Massey embraced a "progressive sense of place" that refused the tendency to view place as self-contained. Massey argued that places are the result of various flows. Building on Massey's ideas, later scholars embraced the mobilities turn that argued that place cannot be understood without understanding movement (Sheller and Urry, 2006). Rather than view travel as "dead time" (Green, 2002), mobilities scholars argue that mobility is an essential element that shapes how people experience place. Places are not merely a set of fixed destinations. Places are performances, and part of those performances is mobility.

The spatial and mobilities turns are important for the study of mobile media. People have often used mobile media to shape their experience of movement. They read on trains, they use the Walkman and the iPod to create "mobile media sound bubbles" (Bull, 2004), and they use mobile phones to engage with distant others while mobile. Critics have argued that mobile media can detract from people's sense of place because people engage more with their media than they do with their surroundings (Gergen, 2002). What unites the book, the Walkman, the iPod, and the mobile phone is that they all introduce a layer of mediation that is external to people's experience of place. A narrative of a novel or a song played through headphones remains the same regardless of the place in which it is experienced.

Locative media alter the relationship between mobile media and place, which is key to understanding their social impacts. People still use smartphones to mediate their experience of mobility, but they do so by interacting with information that is part of that place and forming hybrid spaces in which digital information and physical space merge (Gordon and de Souza e Silva, 2011). In these hybrid spaces, the digital influences experiences of place, but places also influence experiences of the digital. This co-construction of place and locative media is the most relevant shift from older forms of mobile media to the locative media discussed throughout this book. To best understand the social impacts of locative media, it is necessary to analyze how they impact people's experience of place and mobility. How place is experienced matters. And experiences of place cannot be separated from the different technologies used to mediate mobility.

3

The Infrastructure of Locative Media

I bought my first smartphone in 2009. By contemporary standards, the phone's hardware was buggy and slow, the data connection was not fast, the selection of applications was limited, and the phone had trouble getting an accurate GPS signal. The smartphone still felt like magic to me: I could access the Internet from seemingly anywhere and was no longer tied to an Ethernet cable or the limited reach of a Wi-Fi connection. I could see my exact physical location as a dot on my screen. I could download applications that did everything from finding restaurants to telling me how far I hiked. It never occurred to me to really think about how my smartphone worked. Though they may have been invisible to me as an end-user, the different elements of my first smartphone – especially the location awareness, the mobile broadband, and the app store – each had their own history.

People tend to ignore what goes on in the background when they use technologies. They focus more on what technologies do than on how they work, a tendency Bruno Latour (1987) calls the "black boxing" of technology. The tendency to neglect the technologies that make user practices possible is not an inherent weakness in media studies research. Researchers can study how people construct identity on Facebook without discussing the size of Facebook's servers; researchers can talk about the social practices of mobile map users without explaining how GPS works. End-users rarely pay attention to the elements necessary to power their Internet connection, connect their phone calls, or provide their electricity (Blum, 2013).

However, analyses of emerging media can benefit from understanding technological developments. This chapter examines three developments necessary for contemporary location-based services: location awareness, the mobile Internet, and app stores. The next section details how GPS works and then explains other location methods, including cellular triangulation and Wi-Fi-based location. The chapter then gives background on how complicated it can be to understand the "generations" of mobile networks and concludes by discussing the two most popular smartphone operating systems – Android and iOS – and explaining how the creation of mobile app stores was essential to the popularization of location-based services.

Technologies do not determine behavior. Enabling commercial access to GPS and mobile broadband did not make people start using location-based services. Nevertheless, while avoiding technological determinism, it is fair to point out that certain forms of media are not possible without specific technologies, and communication media do indeed shape behavior. To understand how and why location-based services developed the way they did, analyses can benefit from examining how broader technological developments made the applications discussed in later chapters possible.

Location awareness

Almost all contemporary smartphones come equipped with a Global Positioning System (GPS) receiver. GPS is a series of 24 satellites the US Department of Defense launched into orbit around the earth. Scientists began developing GPS in the early 1970s under the name NAVSTAR-GPS, but the first test satellites were not launched until 1978, and the final satellite (the 24th) in the original system was launched in 1994 (Rip and Hasik, 2002). GPS was not the first series of navigation satellites used by the US military. The US launched its first satellite in 1958, one year after Russia launched *Sputnik 1*. Then in the 1960s the US developed the TRANSIT system that became the first functional example of a satellite-based navigation system (Howell, 2013). Physicist Robert J. Danchik (1988) called TRANSIT "arguably the largest step in navigation since the development of the ship-board chronometer" (p. 18), and the system was active until 1996 when it was finally fully replaced by GPS.

By the 1990s, GPS was functional and not fundamentally different from the system used today. One major difference concerned who could get an accurate signal. The system was designed with a feature called Selective Availability (SA) that introduced deliberate errors into the signal received by non-military receivers. SA was turned off in 1990 during the Gulf War because there were not enough military receivers, so troops occasionally used civilian receivers. The feature was then rein-stated on July 1, 1991, and remained turned on until President Bill Clinton issued a directive on May 1, 2000, that turned off the feature permanently. As described by spatial scientist Dennis Milbert, using an American football analogy, "with SA activated, you really only know if you are on the field or in the stands [whereas] with SA switched off, you know which yard marker you are standing on" (quoted in Monmonier, 2002: 15). Literally overnight, turning off the feature changed typical accuracy from around 50m to 3m on a clear day. It is not an overstatement to say that if the US government had maintained SA, the types of locative media used today would not exist.

A description of what happens when someone waits for their phone to get a GPS signal can show how this works in practice. GPS consists of 24 satellites that circle the earth and beam signals to receivers on the ground, and distance is calculated by measuring exactly how long it takes the signal to reach the receiver. The system is designed so that four satellites are ideally visible from any point on earth at any given time. The signals are then used in a calculation called trilateration to pinpoint the receiver's physical location by comparing its distance to at least three satellites, the minimum necessary to get a fully accurate location (Monmonier, 2002). As this rather complicated process suggests, the GPS satellites feature precise atomic clocks able to measure the exact time it takes for the signal to travel to the receiver. Consequently, when someone pulls up an application that says something like "waiting for GPS signal" what is actually happening is that the device waits for signals that travel at the speed of light from multiple satellites and then uses trilateration to pinpoint the location of the receiver.

While people often use GPS as shorthand for describing how mobile phones establish location, phones also use two other methods: cellular triangulation and Wi-Fi access. One of the earliest forms of location awareness was cellular triangulation. Cellular triangulation is not as accurate as GPS, but depending on a variety of factors, it will provide a usable location. Cellular triangulation works on a fairly similar principle to GPS satellites. The network of cell towers for placing calls is dense in many areas and designed to overlap so that there are few gaps between cell-tower coverage (Agar, 2005). Ideally, someone relying on cell-tower triangulation is within range of three or more towers, which allows for a rough calculation of the device's location based on its position relative to multiple towers. While cellular triangulation is not always accurate enough to establish a usable location for location-based services, the US National Security Agency relies on cell towers to collect location information from millions of mobile phones (Gellman and Soltani, 2013). Computer scientist Matt Blaze (2012) pointed out that improvements in cellular triangulation and an increase in the density of cell towers now mean that in some cases triangulation can approach the accuracy of GPS.

A more accurate form of non-GPS location information comes from the location of Wi-Fi hotspots (this is how an iPad determines location). Companies such as Google, Apple, Skyhook Wireless, and Microsoft have compiled huge databases of the location of different Wi-Fi hotspots. One example is Google's use of its fleet of Streetview cars to collect the location of Wi-Fi routers and add their locations to a huge database used by Google Location Services.[1] Now Google also uses Google Location Services to anonymously collect Wi-Fi location from all Android phones unless users turn off this feature. Google is certainly not alone in collecting this type of data. Apple has also built a huge database of Wi-Fi hotspots it uses to improve location services on Apple products, and Skyhook is a company that has collected data on millions of Wi-Fi access points to offer what its website calls the "the fastest, most precise location services." Because Wi-Fi location services compare a phone's location to the Wi-Fi access points within range, the higher the number of nearby Wi-Fi hotspots the more accurate the location information. Wi-Fi location can now often provide location information that is nearly as usable as a GPS signal.

The processes described above obviously require a significant amount of infrastructure. When someone includes longitude and latitude in the metadata of a photo or tracks a route on a mapping application, a variety of physical materials are involved in the process that must work properly. The GPS satellites must maintain their precise orbit and beam a clear signal to the receiver, and the servers that host the huge amount of Wi-Fi location data must be able to communicate with the mobile device. If these material processes do not work, location-based services become more or less useless. The mobile applications cannot locate the mobile device and cannot transmit information about one's location. The tendency to view these information flows as dematerialized, as occurring somehow independently of physical infrastructure, was popular in the early understandings of the Internet I discussed in chapter 1 (Hayles, 1999). But it is important to remember that each time someone uses an application like Foursquare or Yelp, satellites beam signals from space or the phone interacts with distant servers hosting Wi-Fi location data. Of course, providing location information is only one part of the backbone of location-based services. Another key element is the mobile broadband connection that allows the mobile device to communicate with those servers to calculate Wi-Fi location.

The generations of mobile networks

First-generation mobile networks were analog. Second-generation (2G) mobile networks moved from analog to digital, introducing both SMS and mobile data connections. Data speeds increased as 2G was upgraded to 2.5G, which added packet switching and led to services like the Wireless Application Protocol (WAP). WAP was a collection of various mobile Internet standards that enabled mobile phones to access email, download music and ringtones, and retrieve stock prices and weather reports. WAP was heavily promoted in the early 2000s by companies such as Nokia, but "struggled to fulfill the expectations" (Schmiedl, Siedl, and Temper, 2009: 1). Part of the reason for WAP's failure to achieve widespread adoption was that it offered a watered-down version of the Internet: "Due to the lack of bandwidth and the limited processing power of mobile phones at that time, [WAP] did not provide direct access to regular websites but only to a limited set of information especially formatted for the used technology" (Schmiedl et al., 2009: 1).

While WAP was eventually "widely derided as a flop" (Goggin, 2006: 165), a similar mobile data service called i-mode became popular in Japan and eventually spread to 17 other countries. The i-mode service was released in 1999 by Japanese carrier NTT Docomo, and media researcher Gerard Goggin (2006) argued that i-mode's most significant innovation was its "development of audiences and payment systems for content over mobile phones" (p. 167). Use of i-mode made it simpler for people to purchase content such as music and ringtones and also send mobile email, which became a dominant form of communication for Japanese youth (Ito, Okabe, and Matsuda, 2005).

Despite its popularity, however, in many ways i-mode shared more similarities with WAP than with the more fully realized mobile Internet accessed through contemporary smartphones. Only certain Internet services were offered by i-mode, and people could not just browse the web through i-mode. They were typically constrained to the content offered through the system, and "There is an argument, then, that i-mode merely offers a cut-down, highly commercialized, and, in effect, enclosed instantiation of online cultural domains" (Goggin, 2006: 169). However, despite these limitations, the system did allow for

thousands of do-it-yourself i-mode services that were an important predecessor to today's burgeoning mobile application
culture (Hjorth, 2005).

Even as i-mode was popularizing mobile data in Japan and
WAP was struggling elsewhere, plans were already in place
for third-generation (3G) mobile networks. The term "3G" is a
decidedly amorphous one that "describes a range of telephone
protocols (UMTS, cdma2000 and more) that transmit and
receive data at speeds over the threshold at which certain kinds
of mobile internet experiences become possible, such as audio,
image and video downloads, streaming data, online gaming
and so on" (Wilson, 2006: 229). While the language of mobile
"generations" suggests that each generational jump represents
a break from the past, 3G was more of an evolution than a
revolution (Curwen, 2002). Both 2G and 2.5G networks already
enabled mobile data transfer, but according to the International
Telecommunication Union (ITU), 3G networks would provide
much higher data speeds (ITU, 2011). The expected jump in
data speeds was the focus of many of the utopian discourses
from mobile carriers that imagined a fundamental change in
how people used their mobile phones (Goggin, 2006). As is
often the case with technology adoption, however, actual 3G
adoption came in fits and starts and was initially a gigantic
disappointment.

Third- and fourth-generation mobile networks
In the late 1990s and early 2000s, governments around the
world held auctions to sell spectrum allotted to 3G networks.
The spectrum auction in the UK raised £22.5 billion and
auctions throughout the rest of Europe raised another £37.5
billion (Wilson, 2006). However, it was soon apparent that telecom companies had spent far too much on 3G spectrum, and
business journalist Jeremy Warner (2005) speculated that the
spectrum auctions represented "the biggest misallocation of
capital in the modern corporate age" (para 10). A major part of
the problem was that people were slow to switch to 3G devices

(Nielsen and Fjuk, 2010). The 3G networks did not offer particularly fast data speeds, and "No killer application – or 'killer app' – has done enough to stimulate the widespread replacement of 2G handsets in a saturated European mobile market, let alone a large-scale uptake of the kind of subscription-based services that telcos require to break even on 3G" (Wilson, 2006: 231). These factors, combined with the high data prices telecom companies charged – probably to recoup their huge spectrum investment – led to disappointing sales of 3G-enabled devices.

While 3G adoption remained slow for most of the 2000s, people eventually began using 3G. A 2008 Comscore survey found that 28.4 percent of people in the United States owned a 3G device (this includes all 3G-enabled devices, not just phones) compared to a 28.3 percent rate in the five largest European countries. What stands out in the 2008 Comscore survey is that:

> Total subscribers in the U.S. jumped 80.1 percent compared to the same period in 2007. In Europe, the numbers jumped 46.6 percent; in Spain, 75.4 percent; in Germany, 67.1 percent; in the U.K., 46.1 percent; in France, 41.7 percent; in Italy 24.5 percent. (Duryee, 2008: para. 4)

The increase in 3G adoption coincided with the popularization of smartphone technology; both the iPhone 3G and the first Android smartphone were released in 2008. However, as 3G adoption began to increase, countries had already started planning and developing fourth-generation (4G) mobile networks.

As of 2013, 4G mobile phones are available in multiple countries, including Japan, South Korea, the US, France, and England, and China began selling 4G licenses in December 2013 (Mozur and Luk, 2013). However, pinning down a definition of just what "4G" means can be difficult (Goggin, 2010). The ITU defined 4G in terms of technical specifications and improved data speeds, claiming that 4G networks would enable peak data speeds of 100mb/s for mobile users and 1Gb/s for stationary users. These data speed goals were set forth in a 2008 ITU policy document explaining the technical specifications of IMT-

Advanced (the original 4G standard) (ITU, 2008). However, the definition of 4G only got more complicated from there. Carriers began releasing phones labeled as 4G that operated on different network standards that did not come close to the data speeds set forth by the 2008 ITU document. South Korean carriers began releasing supposedly 4G phones that used Mobile WiMax, Verizon released 4G phones on its LTE (Long-Term Evolution) network, and AT&T and T-Mobile began labeling their HSPA+ network as 4G.

None of these technical standards met the data requirements of the ITU's 2008 definition of 4G, so the ITU eventually just broadened the definition to include a wider range of networks:

> Following a detailed evaluation against stringent technical and operational criteria, ITU has determined that "LTE-Advanced" and "WirelessMAN-Advanced" should be accorded the official designation of IMT-Advanced. As the most advanced technologies currently defined for global wireless mobile broadband communications, IMT-Advanced is considered as "4G", although it is recognized that this term, while undefined, may also be applied to the forerunners of these technologies, LTE and WiMax, and to other evolved 3G technologies providing a substantial level of improvement in performance and capabilities with respect to the initial third generation systems now deployed. (ITU, 2010: para. 8)

ITU's changing definition of 4G throws into question the usefulness of labeling mobile network generations. HSPA+ runs on 3G networks, though with higher data speeds. LTE and WIMAX networks, though different from 3G networks, do not meet the requirements for 4G set forth by the standard setting bodies (Buchanon, 2010). The first actual 4G network, according to ITU's original technical specification, was launched in the summer of 2013 in South Korea (Musil, 2013), but at the time of this writing, 4G has become more of a marketing term than an accurate descriptor of data speed or next-generation networks.

As this section has hopefully made clear, the development of the mobile Internet has been uneven. WAP was widely regarded as a failure while i-mode became a huge success in Japan. Initially 3G was a financial disaster that took years to gain widespread usage. The development of 4G networks promised to enable significantly higher data speeds. What happened instead was an incremental improvement over 3G. Despite the complicated development of mobile networks and the uncertain future of true "next-generation" networks, the history of mobile data is important for understanding the past, present, and future of location-based services. The first chapter explained that location-based services are an extension of the Internet. They require data transfers to work, but unlike web pages, they require mobile coverage because they are services tied to physical movement. Even though mobile network standards may remain hidden to many users, they form the backbone of the mobile applications people access through their smartphones.

The development of significantly faster networks could change the shape of location-based services in the future. A study of LTE data speeds across carriers in the US found that the AT&T LTE network was the nation's fastest with average download speeds of 16.7mbps and average upload speeds of 7.4mbps (Reisinger, 2013). The new LTE-Advanced network in South Korea promises download speeds of up to 150mbps (Musil, 2013). That potential boost in data speed may contribute to location-based services and other mobile applications that look significantly different from what is seen today, just as the jump from the relatively slow data speeds of 2.5G to 3G helped contribute to contemporary mobile applications. People can never truly predict the future of emerging media, but if next-generation networks do begin delivering significantly faster data speeds, there will likely be at least some change to the current mobile application ecosystem.

Open and closed:
Google, Apple, and smartphone technology

Many dates in the history of technology are only recognized as important long after they pass. January 9, 2007, on the other hand, was greeted with immediate fanfare. On that date Apple confirmed the existence of the iPhone, addressing rumors about the device that went all the way back to 1999 when Apple purchased the domain name iPhone.org.[2] The attention was so intense that at one point 6 out of 10 Americans supposedly knew the iPhone's release date (Pilkington and Johnson, 2007). People began camping out at Apple stores days before the phone went on sale on June 29, 2007. The stores opened, and the iPhone sold out immediately, in no small part because of "Apple's phenomenally successful marketing campaign" (Goggin, 2009: 235).

The iPhone was not the first smartphone. In 1992, IBM showed the Simon Personal Communicator at a computer industry trade show and released the device to the public in 1994.[3] The Simon featured calendars, voice calls, email, and a touch-screen interface; however, the device was too bulky and expensive to be widely adopted. In the mid-1990s companies such as Hewlett Packard began working on PDAs and Nokia released a popular series of Nokia Communicator smartphones. In the early 2000s, Ericsson released the Symbian operating system, Microsoft released its first Windows smartphone, Handspring released the Palm OS Treo, and Research in Motion (RIM) released the first in a series of BlackBerry phones.

By 2006, 80 million smartphones were shipped worldwide, and Nokia and RIM dominated the smartphone market (Best, 2007). Just as with early mobile phone adoption in the 1980s (Ling, 2004), smartphones were targeted at businessmen and businesswomen. However, the smartphone landscape began to change with the release of the iPhone in 2007, which did not even run on a 3G network. Goggin (2009) argues that what Apple did most successfully was position the iPhone as a mobile computer that opened up the mobile Internet and provided much simpler access to mobile applications. It did not do many things older smartphones could not; it just did them better and had a much better marketing campaign.

The iPhone cut into RIM's dominance of the smartphone

market in the US and Nokia's dominance worldwide, and Google entered the fray in 2008 when handset manufacturer HTC released the first smartphone running the Android operating system (OS). Google's Android has now become the main competitor of iOS (the iPhone's OS) in the smartphone OS market. Of all smartphones shipped in the third quarter of 2013, 81 percent were Android phones, followed by iOS with 12.9 percent,[4] Microsoft Windows with 3.6 percent, and BlackBerry with 1.7 percent (IDC, 2013).

Google and Apple took different approaches to establishing dominance in the smartphone market. Apple focused on one device: the iPhone. Apple designs each version of the iPhone, controls the manufacture of the iPhone,[5] and develops the operating system that runs on the iPhone. Google instead developed Android: an OS that runs on multiple phones manufactured by various companies, including Samsung, Motorola, HTC, and LG, and these different handset manufacturers use modified versions of Android. Consequently, the business model for Android (which Google gives away for free) and iOS are different, and Google has little control over the modifications manufacturers make to their Android phones.

Android looks a lot like iOS, and Steve Jobs was reportedly furious that Android had copied Apple's design (Isaacson, 2013). Both operating systems focus on mobile applications and both rely on touch-screen devices. However, one of the key differences between the two is that iOS is proprietary while Android is open source.[6] Proprietary software is controlled by the company that creates it and the code is not made available to other developers. Open-source software is powered by code that is then shared with the public; iOS is an example of proprietary software, and Apple has been criticized because the closed nature of the system prohibits people from running applications not approved by Apple unless they "jailbreak" the phone to bypass Apple's controls (Zittrain, 2008). In contrast, Android is based on the open-source Linux Kernel, and users are able to manipulate the code that powers the Android operating system.[7] Most Android phones ship with an interface customized by the handset developer, but people are able to "root" their phones to gain access to the entire Android file system and modify the OS.

While Google emphasizes the open nature of Android (Google, 2013a), "Android is hardly as 'open' or 'free' as is commonly perceived" (Goggin, 2012: 742), Google develops each official version of Android in private and then releases it to the public. This approach is different from other open-source projects, such as Linux or Apache, that draw from a community of developers to collaborate on software projects: "there are strict restrictions on the terms of openness Android offers. Google controls code development as described, with the development of the strategically important elements of the next version kept under wraps" (Goggin, 2012: 746). While a full discussion of the politics of the two major smartphone platforms is outside the scope of this chapter, it is still important to briefly push back against some of the more utopian claims about Android as a democratic, open platform. The next section shows that many of the same criticisms of Android and iOS also apply to their mobile app stores.

App stores and the mobile ecosystem
Apple opened its app store in July 2008, one year after the release of the original iPhone. The app store enabled users to download applications directly to their iPhones, either free of charge or for a fee. However, the original app store was more limited than it is today, with Apple restricting third-party developer access. The initial restrictions led to criticisms of the closed architecture of the app store, and Jonathan Zittrain (2008) argued that the iPhone "is sterile. Rather than a platform that invites innovation, the iPhone comes pre-programmed. You are not allowed to add programs to the all-in-one device that Steve Jobs sells you. Its functionality is locked in" (p. 2). Apple partially addressed this criticism by releasing the iOS Software Development Kit (SDK) on March 6, 2009. The SDK allowed third-party developers to create applications for the iPhone. The opening up of the app store contributed to the phenomenal growth of mobile

applications. While i-mode had already shown the benefits of developing a mobile application ecosystem, "it is really only with the advent of Apple iPhone applications that this aspect [mobile applications] of mobile media – indeed the full-fledged entry of mobile computing – has come to fruition" (Goggin, 2011: 150).

Android also features an app store. Google's app store was released in 2008 and now features over 1,000,000 applications that have been downloaded over 50 billion times (Fiegerman, 2013). While some applications, such as Instagram and Foursquare, were initially released only in the Apple store, most popular applications have an Android counterpart. The significant difference between the two app stores goes back to the open vs. closed models that shape each operating system. Apple requires developers to agree to restrictive terms of service to get their applications distributed in the app store and reserves the power to reject applications. While Apple does have an explicit set of reasons why applications can be rejected (Apple, 2014), developers and researchers have criticized the lack of consistency governing which applications are allowed and which are not (Hestres, 2013). If Apple does reject an application, it cannot be downloaded to an iPhone unless users jailbreak their phone. This control in effect gives Apple the final say over what most iPhone owners can and cannot run on their mobile phones.

The Google app store is billed as the more open of the two, and the ability to bypass application censorship is supposedly one of the major benefits of the open nature of Android (Chen, 2008). As mentioned above, Android users can fairly easily root their phones to run applications not found in the Google app store. In addition, Google is less restrictive about the applications allowed into the app store, though Google makes developers agree to a terms-of-service agreement and restricts certain categories of applications (such as pornographic applications) (Google, 2013b). However, Google's app store falls short of the utopian discourses of openness by which it is often portrayed (Goggin, 2012). Mobile carriers and handset manufacturers have exploited Android's openness to load applications on to phones that cannot be deleted without rooting the phone (basically the equivalent of mobile "bloatware") (Siegler, 2010). Google also allows carriers and handset manufacturers to limit how certain applications run despite the fact that the marketplace prides itself on openness. For example, the Android Skype application was originally only available through Verizon because of a Skype/Verizon partnership, and users could not place calls over Wi-Fi (S. Weintraub, 2010). Carriers also got Google to crack down on applications that enabled people to "tether" their phones to use their phones as Wi-Fi hotspots (Isaac, 2011). Possibly most significantly, Google made most of the Google applications – such as the Google Play Store, Google Hangouts, Google Calendar, and Google Music – proprietary, abandoning the previously open versions. By closing off the code to the Google applications that form a significant part of the Android ecosystem, Google has in effect limited developers' ability to move away from Google's control and develop truly open forms of Android. If developers decide to abandon Google's "official" version of Android, Google can then ban access to Google applications, requiring the device to use alternative versions and an alternative app store (Amadeo, 2013). These examples suggest that the openness of Android may end up giving more power to phone manufacturers and carriers than consumers.

The politics of app stores will continue to be important. As Brian Chen (2011) pointed out, app stores have had a major impact on how people access content by centralizing applications in one place. Some tech writers have even argued that applications will slowly replace the more open Web (C. Anderson and Wolff, 2010). While that might be an overstatement, mobile applications will continue to be "an important new cultural platform for mobiles" (Goggin, 2011: 155). Importantly, app stores have been essential to the popularization of location-based services. Many of the applications examined in the following chapters would likely not exist if app stores did not provide distribution channels through which people can find the applications and run them on smartphones. So the politics of app stores matter for the future of location-based services. It matters that Google and Apple control which applications can be downloaded to phones and that carriers and manufacturers can influence what mobile applications are allowed to do. This commercial control throws into question the usefulness of mobile applications as a cultural form that can be adopted for progressive rather than just commercial interests (Goggin, 2012). While this book focuses mainly on commercial applications, it is important to recognize the importance of app stores as a distribution channel while also acknowledging how limitations may shape the development of future mobile applications, including future location-based services.

Conclusion

This chapter examined three elements that played a significant role in shaping contemporary location-based services: location awareness, mobile Internet, and app stores. People rarely think about the underlying technologies that power their media. The location awareness of smartphones is a prime example. This chapter discussed how phones establish location by explaining how GPS, Wi-Fi location, and cellular triangulation work before moving on to a discussion of the "generations" of mobile networks. The mobile Internet has an interesting history filled with successes and failures. Early mobile data standards like WAP were widely regarded as a failure in Europe and the United States, while i-mode was widely adopted in Japan. Though 3G mobile data was seen by carriers as the future of mobile communication, people were slow to adopt 3G-enabled devices. They eventually did, but by that point, planning had already begun for 4G networks.

The history of 4G shows how complicated it can be to understand mobile telephony in terms of "generations." The original technical specifications the ITU set for 4G aimed for data speeds significantly higher than the speeds actually seen on supposed 4G networks. In fact, what consumers now know as 4G networks do not meet the original 4G standards. The ITU had to change the definition of 4G to include all the networks carriers had already labeled with the title. Consequently, 4G has become more of a marketing term than an actual "generation" of mobile networks, and the future of next-generation networks remains unclear. That future does matter, however. Location-based services rely on data to work, and the jump in data speeds made possible by 3G (and now 4G) mobile networks made contemporary location-based services possible. Significant increases in data speeds of true next-generation networks may lead to new possibilities for the design of mobile applications.

The final section of the chapter discussed smartphones and app stores. Smartphone technology existed as far back as the mid-1990s, but it was not until the release of the original Apple iPhone in 2007 that people began widely adopting smartphones. Apple's main competitor in the smartphone OS market is now Google. Interestingly, Apple and Google took different approaches to smartphone dominance. Apple focused on one device: the iPhone. Google created an OS that runs on phones created by various handset manufacturers. Google also adopted an open-source approach to Android, though as I argued above, Android's openness is often overstated.

The differences in Apple and Google's approaches also affect their app stores, which are key to the adoption of location-based services. App stores provide a centralized distribution channel where people can find applications and download them to their smartphones. Apple's app store is more restrictive, limiting the applications people can download to their phones. If Apple does reject an application, people basically cannot access it unless they bypass Apple's control. Google's app store also features some restrictions, but it tends to be more open than Apple's store. Once again, however, the openness of the Android app store is often overstated, and carriers and handset manufacturers are often able to exploit Android's openness.

The central argument of this book is that smartphones as locative media impact how people experience place and merge the digital and physical. They do so in part through a combination of the three technical elements detailed in this chapter. Location services are what enable smartphones to be located in physical space, mobile data are what allows for information about one's surroundings to be transmitted to the smartphone, and mobile app stores are the central point of distribution for the location-based services discussed in the following chapters. Without these elements, the merging of the physical and digital in contemporary hybrid spaces would not occur as it does now. As chapters 4–6 discuss, location-based mobile applications have already begun to impact how people experience place and mobility, and they will continue to do so. Consequently, it is important to understand how these applications work and question the future of application stores as digital marketplaces.

4

Wayfinding through Mobile Interfaces

Most people can picture a map of their surrounding space. They can imagine the best routes to get to their favorite restaurant, figure out the cardinal direction of landmarks, and draw a rough sketch of at least the major roads in their city or town. If they own a smartphone, their phone can do all those things as well. Their smartphone can locate them in physical space using the techniques discussed in chapter 3 and display their approximate position on a variety of mapping applications. These applications can then provide people with walking or driving routes to destinations or spatially display nearby points of interest, depending on their search terms. The smartphones can track their progress as a dot on a map as they travel to reach those points of interest. These maps are one of the earliest examples of location-based services, and mobile maps continue to be some of the most widely used mobile applications.

Maps are one of the more important technologies in human history. They play a significant role in how the world is viewed, divided, and understood. Wars have been fought over lines on maps, and thinking about a relatively young nation like Kosovo shows just how socially constructed maps can be.[1] The simple act of drawing a circle around Kosovo and establishing it as a nation on world maps is the result of years of struggle, war, and debate. And maps are also shaped by national interests. Google provides a different map in India than in China. The Indian map displays the Arunchal Pradesh region as part of India; the Chinese version displays most of the territory as part of China (Ribeiro, 2009).[2] As geographer Doreen Massey (2005) wrote, "a map of a geography is no more that geography – or that space – than a painting of a pipe is a pipe" (p. 106).[3] Maps do not represent a simple reality (Farman, 2010).[4] They "present the accumulated thought and labour of the past" (Pickles, 2004: 60).

Mapping is key to much of this book. Chapter 5 examines the mapping of social networks; chapter 6 examines the mapping of texts and memories. This chapter analyzes location-based services from a wayfinding perspective and investigates how the ability to map routes and places on smartphones impacts how people navigate their surrounding space. The analysis is important for understanding location-based services because Google Maps is one of the most popular mobile applications in the world (McClellan, 2013), and in the United States 50 percent of all mobile phone users (not just smartphone users) access maps and directions on their phones (Duggan, 2013). Maps shape the way people know the world, and with smartphones many individuals now map more information than ever before. Much of that information relies on teams of users, and the next section examines different mapping applications and point-of-interest applications like Yelp and focuses on the social data they draw from to power their maps and lists of locations. The chapter then analyzes how mobile mapping may contribute to new forms of mobile coordination while also impacting people's ability to form cognitive maps. Maps are an old technology; as a much newer technology, mobile mapping applications have already begun to impact how people represent and navigate their surrounding space, an issue explored throughout the rest of this chapter.

The social production of mobile maps

Almost every smartphone comes with a pre-installed mapping application. Android phones have Google Maps pre-installed; iPhones features Apple Maps. Windows phones come with Bing Maps. All of these phones assume people will use them for navigation, and short of rooting or jailbreaking the phone, users cannot remove these navigation applications. The pre-installed mapping applications have obvious roots in in-car GPS devices, which were one of the first popular examples of location-based services. Mapping applications can also be traced back to online mapping sites. In the 1990s, the website Mapquest showed that people would use the Internet to find places and get directions. Google Maps has now become the most popular mapping website, and the Google Maps application, along with Bing Maps and Apple Maps, enables people to pinpoint their location, look at a map of their surrounding space, and access turn-by-turn directions. These applications do more than provide directions. They also display different types of information depending on users' search terms: if people search for "Indian restaurants" on Google Maps, they are presented with markers placed on a map of their surrounding space. They can also search for specific place names and get driving or walking directions from their location to the places returned in the search.

Navigation applications are only one of many different types of location-based services that can map information and impact individual wayfinding practices. Another category of applications focuses specifically on points of interest. Applications like Gasbuddy map the locations of nearby gas stations. The Wikipedia application provides maps of nearby Wikipedia articles. Applications like Urban Spoon and Yelp focus on reviews and maps of nearby businesses. These applications often display information in both list form, which provides the distance to a location, and map form. Basically, any digital information that includes locational metadata can be mapped, ranging from pictures uploaded to applications like Instagram to the location of people who check in on Facebook (Hochman and Manovich, 2013), two examples discussed in more detail in chapters 5 and 6.

Most of the information found in location-based services like Yelp, Urbanspoon, and Instagram is user-generated. On Yelp, for example, people write reviews of locations and they also can add locations to the database and add phone numbers and addresses. The information is social, and returning to the concept of hybrid space introduced in chapter 1 (de Souza e Silva, 2006), applications like Yelp are a clear example of the merging of the physical, digital, and social. While these applications are not strictly mapping applications, they do provide users with maps and do enable them to spatially represent nearby restaurants and reviews uploaded from other users. The user-generated location-based content can then impact the mobility choices of someone else using the application to find new places and make wayfinding decisions.

The social elements of popular navigation applications like Google Maps are less obvious. Returning to the introduction of this chapter, all maps are socially constructed representations (Wood, 1992). They present certain types of information at certain scales; mapmakers always make choices. The information displayed on Google Maps features choices made by the people who create the algorithm and power the site. Interestingly, however, a community of volunteers operating in the background create and update some of the information found on Google Maps. If users opens up a web browser and go to Google Maps, the lower right-hand corner of the map includes small print telling them to "Edit in Google Map Maker" or "Report a Problem." If they click on the edit option, they go to a screen that asks them to "Enrich Google Maps with your local knowledge." This feature is called Google Map Maker. People using Google Map Maker can add points of interest by adding a restaurant's address as a marker on the map and updating information about locations on the map. Edits are then added to the database and wait to be approved by other members of the Google Map Maker community. Once the edits are approved, they become part of the Google Map seen by all users. Google still has the final say on what appears on Google Maps, but the Google Map Maker community is an important reminder that – even on applications in which the social elements are not obvious – users often contribute much of the data that keep mobile maps current and useful.

Other navigation applications are more focused on social elements than Google Maps. The largest open-source, community-generated mapping service is OpenStreetMap (OSM), which was created in 2004 by Steve Coast. OSM combines data from users, Geographical Information System (GIS) projects, commercial entities, and government data. Anyone with a user account can add points of interest to the maps and can update errors in street mapping. OSM does not require the same review process as Google Map Maker, meaning that it works more like Wikipedia than Google Map Maker's slower peer-review system. The OSM website also emphasizes that the map is entirely community driven, free for anyone to use, and full of local knowledge contributed by users.

While Google Maps may be a much more popular stand-alone mapping application, OSM forms the backbone of many popular location-based services. OSM's Application Programming Interface (API) is open and free for developers to include in their own applications. Google used to allow access to the Google Maps API free of charge, but in 2012 the company began restricting high-volume users (meaning popular mobile applications) from accessing the API unless they pay for a Maps API for Business account (Google, 2013c). The decision to charge for access to the API led some popular location-based services, such as Foursquare and Wikipedia (Beadon, 2012), to switch to OSM, and some tech writers expect OSM to become more popular as more applications move away from Google Maps (Wilhelm, 2012). Even some parts of Apple Maps are powered by OSM. Whether smartphone users know it or not, they likely have an application on their phone that taps into the OSM mapping community to map information.

The final social navigation application addressed here is the Israeli mapping service Waze. Created in 2006, Waze is a community mapping service that provides navigation and turn-by-turn directions similarly to Google and Apple Maps. Waze relies on people to contribute data, and the application passively collects GPS data from users to provide real-time driving information. If someone using Waze hits traffic on a highway, other Waze users will see the traffic on their Waze map and can change their route accordingly. People can also edit roads to keep the map up-to-date, and most importantly, they can report traffic accidents in real time. Rio de Janeiro and cities in Florida even formed a partnership with Waze that allowed the cities to access Waze's real-time transportation data and accident reporting to help improve traffic (Olson, 2014). The crowdsourced nature of Waze and the lack of peer-review barriers for editing the maps have contributed to Waze's increasing popularity, and as of November 2013, more than 20 million people had downloaded the application. Waze is not the only navigation application to provide real-time traffic data; Google Maps does as well by passively collecting location information from Android phones. But Waze encourages people to actively contribute that data and to report road conditions. Unsurprisingly considering its long history of acquiring startups, Google purchased Waze in June, 2013, and has already begun to incorporate user-generated Waze data into the Google Maps traffic feature (Versace, 2013).

The social nature of these mapping applications stands in contrast to traditional maps, which were typically a technology controlled by the powerful (Pickles, 2004). People can now contribute information and alter the maps they use in ways that were not previously possible. However, despite the growth of user-generated content, a few huge companies still control the vast majority of digital maps. Google is now the leading mapping service in the world and spends over $1 billion a year on Google Maps, and some critics fear the consequences of giving huge corporations so much control over the ability to map information (Wroclawski, 2014). Those fears became more pertinent when Google bought Waze, further reducing the number of popular mobile mapping services. Nothing is stopping a company like Google from allowing sponsored spatial searches that display certain locations while hiding others, and that is part of the reason OSM is such an important project. OSM focuses on collaborative mapping, and unlike with Google Map Maker and now Waze, the user-generated content is not controlled by one company.[5]

While people should remain concerned about allowing a few private companies to control so much mapping data, those concerns do not change the fact that these maps are still more social than ever before. These social applications make contributing spatial information easier in much the same way as the growth of the World Wide Web enabled people to produce and share new types of content (Jenkins, Ford, and Green, 2013), and they show the value of encouraging people to play an active role in shaping the maps they use (Gordon and de Souza e Silva, 2011). The social contributions show how these applications fit with the concepts of hybrid space, and they also can impact the mobility practices of users, a topic discussed in the next section. If Waze users see that traffic is bad on a highway, they may change their route immediately. People using Yelp may find new restaurants that were previously invisible to them until they showed up on their smartphone screen. If location-based services can become a "lens" through which people view their surrounding space (Dourish and Bell, 2011), then the social contributions of users can have a significant impact on how people interact with their surrounding space and how they coordinate their mobility practices.

Mobile wayfinding and flexible alignment

The mobile phone altered both the place and time of technologically mediated communication. With landline phones, people call places; with mobile phones, people call people (Wellman, 2002). Mobile phones usage meant people could be reached almost anywhere at any time and were no longer required to wait in specific places for people to call. The reconfiguration of both the space and time of communication contributed to new forms of "connected presence" (Licoppe, 2004) in which people maintain constant contact with absent others through text messaging and voice calls in ways that were previously impossible. Sociologist Rich Ling (2004) even went so far as to argue that mobile phones lessened the importance of "mechanical time" because they made time more flexible: "Arguably the greatest social consequence arising from the adoption of the mobile telephone is that it challenges mechanical timekeeping as a way of coordinating everyday activities" (Ling, 2004: 69). This reshaping of time had major social impacts, leading to new forms of "microcoordination" (Ling, 2004), which refers to people's ability to use the mobile phone to change plans while mobile. Before mobile phones, people had to establish plans before leaving the house and then meet at a specific place at a specific time. Mobile communication impacted these planning practices by making planning more flexible and making it possible to change plans at the last minute.

Mobile maps may now have a similar impact on people's planning practices. An illustration of three different situations can show how. The first involves a person walking around with a paper map. People with paper maps are able to plan routes using the map, but they typically must know the general location of their final destination before heading out. A paper map of a city will not often tell people the location of specific offices or restaurants. They must already know where those locations are before leaving the house or else they will not be able to plan routes using the map. An online mapping site, in contrast, will provide routes to specific locations, but again people must plan those routes and print the maps before heading out. They must already know their final destination before leaving the house. Both the paper map and the online map require people to plan a path beforehand, and if they choose to go somewhere else, the map will only be minimally useful in showing them the way.

Mobile wayfinding applications can impact the planning necessary to navigate physical space; they can change both the place and time of mapping. People using the Google Maps application can decide at the last minute to go to a different place and then find a route on their phone. They can get to a restaurant, see there is a long wait, and then pull up a map of nearby restaurants using Yelp. They can use a mobile tour-guide application like Guidebook to see maps of nearby historical sites rather than planning their routes before leaving the hotel. All these examples of mapping can potentially impact how people coordinate and plan, and point-of-interest applications like Yelp or many other review-based applications can impact the spatial and temporal rhythms of information retrieval. A group of friends meeting in a downtown area do not necessarily need to do research before heading out. They do not have to find the best bars or print out maps of where a certain restaurant is. They can instead agree to meet in one place and then use their smartphones to retrieve information about their surrounding space.

Danish researcher Troels Bertel (2013a) found examples of this realignment of planning and coordination in his interviews with Danish smartphone users. He described situations in which his research participants were able to change plans on the fly because they could use smartphones to retrieve spatial information, and he called this shift in information retrieval "flexible alignment." People are able to exert more flexibility over their daily events because they are able to look up mapping information while mobile, just as mobile phone users can flexibly rearrange schedules because they can contact distant others. Flexible alignment refers to many different types of smartphone information retrieval, ranging from updated Facebook events to the most recent bus schedules. Many of the examples Bertel details – such as getting directions to a friend's house and looking at maps of weather systems – focus specifically on mapping, and his concept of flexible alignment shows how mobile maps are an extension of the types of microcoordination identified by Ling a decade earlier. People are less reliant on planning because they are able to turn to their phones for spatial information when they want to change their plans. As the next section shows, the reliance on mobile mapping not only impacts people's planning practices; it can also impact the cognitive maps people develop about the places they move through.

Spatial cognition and mobile maps

Geographers and environmental psychologists have studied how people develop cognitive maps – which are "a mental representation, or set of representations, of the spatial layout of the environment " (Montello and Freundschuh, 2005: 8) – and how different wayfinding methods affect the acquisition of spatial knowledge. Research on emerging navigation technologies initially examined in-car GPS displays and their effect on how people moved through space. For as convenient as these devices can be, the use of in-car GPS can have drawbacks when compared to other forms of navigation, and research has shown that people who used in-car GPS showed lower levels of spatial-knowledge acquisition compared to people who played a more active role in mapping their routes (Bakdash, Linkenauger, and Proffitt, 2008).

Researchers have extended this line of inquiry to examine how mobile mapping applications impact how people relate to the places they navigate. One of the most cited studies to examine wayfinding through mobile maps was a 2008 article in the *Journal of Environmental Psychology* by Ishikawa and colleagues (2008). The study used an interesting methodology to analyze how people perceive and remember place differently when using direct experience, paper maps, or mobile maps. The researchers divided participants into three groups and asked the groups to walk from one place to another. The first group walked the route with a guide and then walked the route alone. The second group used a paper map of the area, planned a path, and then walked that route. The third group used a mobile phone that featured a mapping application. The group members could see their location on the phone's interface and were provided with a route to travel in an almost identical fashion to contemporary mobile navigation applications. The researchers measured the time it took each group to travel to the final destination and then asked participants to estimate the distance they traveled, estimate the cardinal direction of landmarks, and sketch a map of the place they had just walked through.

Their study found the mobile-map group members performed worst on both the travel time and spatial recall parts of the study. They took longer to navigate the space than the group that had direct experience through the guided tour and the group that mapped the route with a paper map. The mobile-map group participants also gave less accurate estimations of the distance they traveled, were less able to recall the route they took, and did worst when describing details of the streets they moved through. As the authors summarize, "These results show that the GPS-based navigation system affects the user's wayfinding behavior and spatial understanding differently than do the maps and direct experience" (p. 80).

Ishikawa and colleagues' work and other studies that reported similar findings consistently show that mobile maps can decrease the information people process and remember about their surrounding space (Münzer, Zimmer, Schwalm, Baus, and Aslan, 2006; Willis, Hölscher, Wilbertz, and Li, 2009). For example, Willis and colleagues (2009) also compared different groups and found that mobile-map users were less able to estimate the distance they traveled and the relational position of four different destinations. The researchers also found that mobile-map users were less able to develop accurate cognitive maps of the space they traversed than the groups that used traditional maps to plan routes. What these studies do not necessarily do is answer the question of why mobile map users show lower degrees of spatial knowledge acquisition, though researchers have theorized about the reasons. Likely the most consistent reason presented in the research is that people who follow routes on their phone pay less attention to their surrounding space (Ishikawa et al., 2008; Willis et al., 2009). They engage more with their mobile phone screen than their environment, a point that echoes the criticisms of earlier mobile media discussed in chapter 2.

Another reason people may engage less with their surroundings when using mobile maps involves the less active role people play in their wayfinding practices. The act of planning a route using a paper map requires people to consider alternative routes, view a representation of a place in its entirety, and then actively make a mobility choice (Ishikawa et al., 2008). After making that choice, people must engage visually with information in that place (e.g., street signs and landmarks) to follow the route they planned. Mobile maps require less active participation. Users are provided with a suggested route and then given their location on the map. They are able to track their progress as they follow the route. Willis and colleagues (2009) write that "A mobile map with automated position information (i.e., self-localization) essentially enables and possibly even encourages someone using it to switch off and to become the passive receiver of information, and as such does not support learning in a constructive manner" (p. 108). Participants in these studies offloaded the cognitive task of wayfinding to their mobile device, just as writers may spend less time learning how to spell certain words because their word-processing programs alert them to misspellings. The research as a whole has led one research team to write that mobile maps have "effectively become too usable, such that navigators are depending on them to the detriment of their geographic knowledge and orientation skills" (Waters and Winter, 2011: 103).

The studies discussed above view the lack of active participation and the transformation of the walker into a passive receiver of information as a problem. The criticisms are valid and suggest that location-based services, despite how they differ from other mobile media in the ways they access information from surrounding space, can draw people's attention more to the representation of a place on their smartphone screen than their actual physical surroundings. However, the offloading of cognitive effort to mobile mapping applications raises more interesting questions than simply whether this is good or bad; it raises fundamental questions about why people use technology.

Mobile wayfinding and the offloading of cognition

People often rely on various technologies to store their memories (Garde-Hansen, Hoskins, and Reading, 2009). This is not new. Ancient Greek philosopher Socrates famously criticized the technology of the written word for allowing people to write things down rather than remember them. Diaries and scrapbooks enabled people to mediate their memories by storing them elsewhere (Good, 2013). Increasingly, digital media technologies also impact memory practices (Garde-Hansen et al., 2009). Email services store all email correspondence. Google and Wikipedia enable easy access to information, making it less necessary to remember specific facts. Mobile phone contact lists decrease the need to remember phone numbers. These examples show how users turn to various technologies for the process of remembering, just as the authors cited earlier fear in the case of wayfinding and mobile maps. Mobile map users rely on their smartphones to provide them with accurate directions, lessening the need to form cognitive maps, remember routes, and actively plan their own routes. Many people can probably think of a time their smartphone died and they had no idea how to get where they wanted to go.

Rather than make blanket evaluative statements about whether mobile maps are good or bad, people can benefit from exploring how these applications fit within the context of contemporary theories of technology. Influential cognitive social theories tended to use what philosopher Andrew Pickering (2010) calls the Modern Self as the starting point for understanding how individuals think and act. Often influenced by seventeenth-century philosopher René Descartes, the typical model was to understand cognition as if it is contained within the individual. However, an influential set of postcognitive theories have taken different approaches to understanding how humans learn and act. Theories such as Actor-Network Theory, Activity Theory, and Phenomenology all view cognition as distributed throughout the environment. While these theories are all significantly different, "A major source of agreement among the postcognitivist theories is the vital role of technology in human life" (Kaptelinin and Nardi, 2006: 197). As theories of technology, postcognitive approaches can provide a conceptual understanding of what happens when people use mobile maps as wayfinding tools.

The key link between these different theories is that they believe cognition is not contained within the individual; instead postcognitive theories are critical of the idea of the Modern Self and believe cognition is distributed through networks of humans and technologies. For example, influential Phenomenologist Maurice Merleau-Ponty (1962) discussed how, for a blind man using a cane, the cane "has ceased to be an object for him and is no longer perceived for itself" (p. 143). The cane becomes an extension of the man in the physical environment. Activity theorists have examined how people distribute cognition and accomplish goal-directed behavior by turning to tools (Engestrom, 1991; Kaptelinin, Nardi, and MacCaulay, 1999). Actor-Network Theory takes a more extreme approach, arguing that a boundary cannot be drawn between individuals and their tools because action can only be understood by examining the sociotechnical network as a whole (Akrich, 1992; Latour, 1987, 2005). These approaches all radically reformulate the understanding of cognition; if cognition is distributed among humans and tools, then cognitive practices change as tools change. Consequently, postcognitive theories provide a different way of looking at the results discussed in the studies of mobile mapping. Rather than viewing individuals as acting alone in forming cognitive maps, people can instead view individuals and the mobile mapping applications as part of a network.

Viewing the human and the technology as a network rather than two distinctly separate entities opens up the opportunity for understanding mobile mapping as part of what is called "transactive memory." Transactive memory refers to a "combination of memory stores held directly by individuals and the memory stores they can access because they know someone who knows that information" (Sparrow, Liu, and Wegner, 2011: 776). Transactive memory involves people offloading their memory into their environment, and that environment includes people (two people can form what is called a transactive memory system) and various technologies. A husband may rely on his wife to remember their daughter's address; the wife may rely on her husband to remember their son's birthday. A woman might not remember the date of an upcoming event because she relies on her planner as a transactive memory network. In a study of how the Internet affects memory, psychologists Betsy Sparrow, Jenny Liu, and Daniel M. Wegner (2011) found that people used the Internet as a form of transactive memory because when they thought answers were being stored online they tended to remember where they could find specific facts rather than the facts themselves. As the authors point out, "These results suggest that processes of human memory are adapting to the advent of new computing and communication technology" (p. 778). Their findings can also be applied to the use of mobile mapping applications. People may remember less about the routes they take, but that is because of a transactive memory process. They know *where* to find mapping information, so going back to Activity and Actor-Network Theory, the activity of the network changes when people enfold the new tool of mobile mapping into their everyday lives.

People rely on mobile maps as wayfinding tools, and this reliance can decrease their ability to form cognitive spatial maps and recall elements of the places they move through. However, rather than viewing this as inherently negative, postcognitive theories like Activity Theory, Phenomenology, and Actor-Network Theory suggest that this kind of behavior can be found in many interactions with technology. When people use mobile maps, they distribute their cognition into a new type of tool and rely on their smartphones as a form of transactive memory. Just as the written word decreased the importance of remembering oral storytelling and spell check makes it less important to remember which words have double letters, these mapping applications make it less necessary to remember specific routes or places passed through. As with the adoption of any new technology, there is always a trade-off, but returning to the key argument of this book, as tools change, so do interactions with the environment. Locative media provide new ways of seeing and navigating physical space, and the mapping applications discussed above are one of the prime examples of how hybrid spaces have begun to shift how people understand their surroundings.

Conclusion

People now map more information than ever before. They map articles on Wikipedia, reviews on Yelp, gas stations on Gasbuddy. They also carry mobile maps in the palms of their hands. Mobile navigation applications like Google and Apple Maps come pre-installed on smartphones, and they provide people with routes and turn-by-turn directions. This chapter examined mobile maps from a wayfinding perspective, focusing on how mobile mapping impacts how people navigate space and coordinate behavior.

The first section examined various types of mobile applications that impact individuals' wayfinding practices. These include navigation applications as well as point-of-interest applications that map specific types of information. Many of these applications – even corporate navigation applications like Google Maps – draw from user-generated information. The use of user-generated information shows how these applications fit with the concept of hybrid space discussed in chapter 1 (de Souza e Silva, 2006): they merge the social, digital, and physical, and the intertwining of the three can impact how people experience place and coordinate behavior, which was the focus of the second section of this chapter. That section examined how mobile maps can change the place and time of mapping and contribute to new forms of flexible alignment. Flexible alignment refers to the ability to change plans because of smartphone information retrieval (Bertel, 2013a), and mobile mapping may impact coordination practices in much the same way text messaging and voice calls did more than a decade ago.

Finally, this chapter analyzed research on how mobile maps impact how people come to know a place. Research has consistently shown that people who rely on the turn-by-turn directions of mobile maps do not do as well when forming cognitive maps and recalling details of the places they move through (Ishikawa et al., 2008; Willis et al., 2009). These findings have led some to criticize mobile maps for being "too usable" and turning people into passive receivers of information rather than people who actively plan their mobility choices (Waters and Winter, 2011). However, rather than make blanket statements about whether mobile maps are good or bad, this chapter attempted to understand them within the context of postcognitive theories of technology. Postcognitive theories believe that cognition is not contained within the individual; it is instead spread throughout the environment (Kaptelinin and Nardi, 2006). Drawing from postcognitive theories allows individuals to view mobile mapping applications as part of a transactive memory network; people using these applications do not need to form as detailed cognitive maps because they know where to find mapping information.

The reliance on mobile mapping represents an example of how smartphones as locative media can impact how people relate to their surrounding space. As chapter 2 discussed, how people know places and figure out how to navigate their surroundings is an important part of their experience of the everyday. A key argument of this book is that locative media have begun to shift how people understand and negotiate their environment. The ability to map more information than ever before has resulted in new spatial practices by which people are able to remake plans on the fly because they can access spatial information, though they also may become reliant on that spatial information in a way that impacts how they remember and navigate their spaces. Consequently, mobile mapping shows how the merging of physical space with digital information through mobile interfaces has begun to reconfigure people's relationship with the physical world.

5

Location and Social Networks

I was a college freshman when I first got a mobile phone. I remember sitting in the common area of my dorm and talking to my girlfriend back home. I was less than 10 feet away from people with whom I shared a living space, but like many of my friends who were also on their phones, I was more connected to someone 150 miles away. Describing this type of situation, Ichiyo Habuchi (2005) argued that mobile phone users form "telecocoons" to communicate with distant others rather than engage with people nearby. Her concept certainly applies to the social situation of my freshman dorm. My friends and I often used our mobile phones to form telecocoons and connect with people far away rather than talk to the people around us.

While people tend to use their mobile devices to avoid engaging with nearby people (Humphreys, 2005), a few commercial projects in the late 1990s and early 2000s explored how mobile technologies could encourage face-to-face communication. One of the first such examples was a Japanese technology called Lovegety: "the first commercial attempt to take introduction systems away from the desktop and into reality" (Eagle and Pentland, 2004: 3). Lovegety was a stand-alone mobile device that sold for around $25 and became popular in Japan in the late 1990s, and people carried the device with them and received alerts when other Lovegety users were nearby and interested in meeting up (Rheingold, 2002). The proximity-aware features of the system were important predecessors to many of the location-based social applications discussed in this chapter.

Lovegety focused on the near rather than the remote, the present rather than the absent. It connected users to others sharing a physical space and encouraged face-to-face connections, a goal it shared with the first commercial location-sharing service in the US: Dodgeball. Whereas Lovegety was a stand-alone mobile device, Dodgeball relied on the mobile phone and a mass text-messaging system to enable people to share their location with friends. Later mobile applications, called location-based social networks (LBSNs), took advantage of the technological capabilities of newer smartphones to expand upon Dodgeball's location-sharing model. LBSNs like Loopt, Brightkite, Whrrl, Gowalla, Foursquare, and Latitude encouraged people to build social networks and share their physical location. Many LBSN features, such as Foursquare's check-ins, were later incorporated into huge social network sites (SNS) like Facebook. LBSNs and the incorporation of location elements in other SNS represent a relatively new way for people to communicate: they do not just communicate *about* location, they communicate *through* location (Frith, 2014).

Despite much initial hype from articles that labeled LBSNs as "next year's Twitter" (Cashmore, 2009), LBSNs have not made the jump to mainstream adoption. A national survey from the PEW Internet and American Life project even found a decrease in LBSN popularity. The survey found the percentage of smartphone users who checked in on an LBSN decreased from 18 percent in 2012 to 12 percent in 2013 (Zickuhr, 2013). In addition, the most popular LBSN – Foursquare, which has over 45 million users ("About Foursquare," 2014) – moved its location-sharing features to a stand-alone mobile application called Swarm in May, 2014, a tacit acknowledgment that for the company to grow, it had to de-emphasize location sharing and focus on local search.

However, the seeming decline of LBSNs does not mean that people are not using smartphones to share their location. Kathryn Zickuhr, an associate for PEW Research, points out that "It's entirely possible people are shifting from using these check-in services to sharing their location with their friends in other ways, such as sharing their location on social network sites"

(Popkin, 2013: para. 5). Her research showed that 30 percent of adult social media users in the United States now tag posts with location information, and the majority of the increase in users came on sites like Facebook, Instagram, and Twitter (Zickuhr, 2013: 12). In other words, while the use of LBSNs like Loopt and Foursquare has decreased, the amount of location information people share with others has actually increased. As smartphone adoption continues to grow and people become more comfortable with a range of location-based services, location sharing will likely be incorporated into more and more social applications. After all, as mobile media researcher Lee Humphreys (2012) argues, "our increased mobilities call for articulation of our physical locations in new and more frequent ways" (p. 504).

This chapter examines the phenomenon of social location sharing and begins by providing a brief history of the development of commercial LBSNs. While LBSNs have not fully caught on, they are an important development in the history of social media, especially considering that many of their location-sharing features have now been incorporated in larger sites like Facebook. The chapter then focuses on three theoretical areas important to understanding the potential impact of social location sharing: (1) coordinating through location; (2) constructing identity through location; and (3) sharing location and the impact on public space. These issues are addressed through an analysis of published research and qualitative research I performed with Foursquare users during 2011–12 (Frith, 2012a). This chapter does not discuss the privacy concerns associated with location sharing, but the second half of chapter 8 covers social locational privacy. As this chapter shows, location has now become an important piece of social data that people share with others, and now that 30 percent of all social media users in countries such as the United States share location on social media (Zickhur, 2013), it is important to understand how people are using physical places as pieces of digital information they share with their social networks.

A brief history of location-based social networks

Lovegety achieved its brief popularity in Japan in the late 1990s, but the first commercial location-sharing service in the US – Dodgeball – was not released until 2000. Dodgeball did not rely on location-aware technologies to determine location. Instead, people signed up for the service and created lists of friends. They texted their location to a central server, and the service sent their location to their Dodgeball friends. As Lee Humphreys (2007, 2010) showed through her ethnography of Dodgeball users, the service is an early example of how location sharing can impact the ways that people communicate with friends and coordinate behavior.

Dodgeball achieved modest popularity in the early 2000s and was purchased by Google in 2005. By that point, other companies had begun developing LBSNs that took advantage of the new technological capabilities of mobile phones. One of the first such services was Loopt, which was released in 2006 and was featured in an early iPhone commercial.[1] Loopt was followed by other LBSNs, such as Brightkite, Whrrl, and Gowalla, that also enabled people to share their location with their social network. Then in March, 2009, Foursquare was launched at the annual South by Southwest Interactive (SxSWi) festival. Foursquare was not fundamentally different from competing LBSNs. Foursquare users created a network of friends and then shared their location whenever they publicly checked in. The application also included gaming elements such as points and badges, just like other applications such as Gowalla. However, Foursquare was more successful than other LBSNs. Loopt struggled to grow its user base and was acquired by the Green Dot Corporation. Brightkite's developers pulled the application from the Apple store in 2011. Whrrl was purchased in 2011 by Groupon and was slowly phased out. Gowalla was purchased by Facebook in 2011 and ceased operation in 2012. Foursquare continued to grow. As of April 2014, Foursquare had over 45 million users worldwide who had checked in over 5 billion times ("About Foursquare," 2014).

Foursquare was undoubtedly the most popular LBSN; however, the application has moved away from location sharing to focus more on local search and location recommendations, a topic covered in more detail in chapter 7. In May, 2014, Foursquare went so far as to remove the check-in feature from the application and create a stand-alone Swarm application people could use to share location. Foursquare now only features its spatial search function and spatial recommendation notifications. The splitting off of check-ins from the main Foursquare application to the new Swarm application shows why it is important to focus more on practices than the design of individual applications. Applications change, especially in a dynamic field like location-based services. Developing an understanding of why and how people do things like share their location can be more valuable than detailing applications that may not even be available by the time this book is published. That lesson is especially true for social location sharing because huge SNS, such as Instagram and Facebook, now include location sharing, and many people incorporate location into the applications they already use rather than adopt stand-alone LBSNs. Ultimately, by focusing on how and why people share location, this chapter will hopefully be just as applicable to future applications as it is to contemporary applications that include location features.

While an overly specific focus on one application can be limiting, there are times it makes sense to go into some detail on different design approaches. One such case is the difference between the check-ins on the older version of Foursquare and another LBSN that gained some notoriety before being shut down by Google in August, 2013: Latitude. In 2009, Google shut down Dodgeball and released Latitude. Latitude's location-sharing approach was different from Foursquare and Gowalla. With Foursquare, people checked in to locations (they can now do so through the separate Swarm application). The information they shared with their friends was the name of the location (e.g., Big Boss Taproom), not their actual longitude and latitude.

Their location then did not update until they chose to check in to another location. Latitude, on the other hand, tracked physical location (actual coordinates, not the name of locations) in real time if the user turned on that feature. Cramer, Rost, and Holmquist (2011) used Foursquare and Latitude as examples of the two major approaches to location sharing: the check-in model and the location-tracking model.

The check-in model closely follows Dodgeball's text-message-based design and requires people to manually update and share their location. Location tracking is a more passive process; people can choose to let the application run and passively broadcast their physical location. Some location-sharing applications, such as Apple's Find My Friends and Glympse, draw from the location-tracking model. Yet others, such as Facebook's feature that allows people to share their location or Instagram's ability to tag pictures with physical location, draw from the check-in model popularized by Foursquare. Each approach has its advantages. Check-ins give users more control over location sharing, which can help with the concerns about locational privacy discussed in chapter 8 (Cramer et al., 2011). Location tracking has the advantage of being less cumbersome and possibly more accurate because users do not have to manually update their location when they leave a place. These two approaches are worth noting because future location-sharing applications will likely follow one of these two general designs.

Before moving on to cover areas of research relevant to location sharing, it is necessary to include a word of caution. The failure of so many LBSNs like Gowalla, Loopt, and Latitude, the niche status of applications like Find My Friends and Glympse, and Foursquare's de-emphasis of check-ins suggest that location sharing may never enter the mainstream. Danish researcher Troels Bertel's work with Danish youth found that "the practice of checking-in has not become a routinized part of everyday life" (2013b: 89). Bertel's point is an important one because, despite a great deal of attention from the tech press and academic researchers, location sharing is still not an overly common practice and it may never become so. So while location has become an increasingly popular form of information shared on Facebook, Instagram, and other social network sites, researchers must be careful not to overemphasize the importance of social location sharing. That being said, location sharing is still a relevant area of research because even if it remain a relatively niche practice, the finding that 30 percent of social media users share location is not insignificant (Zickuhr, 2013). In addition, it is impossible to predict the future of technology adoption, and people could still develop new ways to use location for social purposes. After all, as Gartner's (2014) Hype Cycle approach to studying technology adoption suggests, new technologies such as LBSNs often face a period of inflated expectations, followed by a period of disillusionment, which is then followed by an increased plateau of productivity. With Foursquare's fissure and other LBSN failures, LBSNs are currently in a period of disillusionment. But location will continue to be used in various applications and that usage will likely increase in the near future.

Coordinating through location

The mobile phone impacted coordination practices by allowing people to change plans while mobile, a topic covered in chapter 4. Coordination can also be impacted by the adoption of social location-sharing applications. Humphreys (2012) defined coordination as "communicative exchanges around organizing and situating our physical selves in relation to one another" (p. 503), and her definition shows why location-sharing applications can impact coordination practices. One reason people share location is to position themselves relationally to the members of their social network. In fact, the relational positioning of mediated location sharing goes back at least as far as the 1990s and the Active Badge system (Dourish and Bell, 2011). Active Badge was a location-tracking system that relied on a series of networked sensors that detected people's locations and shared them with the central system. Active Badge focused on location sharing in office environments, and it operated under the assumption that people could coordinate better if they were made aware of co-workers' location.

Like Active Badge, Lovegety focused on coordination, though of a social rather than professional sort. Lovegety worked in a fundamentally different way from the mobile phone. Mobile phones, as Rich Ling (2004) detailed, are often used to coordinate behavior with absent others. People used Lovegety to find nearby people with whom to interact. However, as Dodgeball later showed, the tendency to use the mobile phone to communicate with the remote rather than the near was not something determined by the phone. Dodgeball showed how people could use text messaging to broadcast their location to friends as a way to coordinate face-to-face communication.

For many of the Dodgeball users Humphreys (2007, 2010) observed and interviewed, the Dodgeball check-in worked as an invitation to engage in further sociability:

> Users would check in to a location on Dodgeball and other users might see that check-in and meet up with them in the neighborhood. Often this would not be at the same venue as the original check-in but would occur in the same general neighborhood. Sometimes people would check into a location not because they wanted to meet up there but to indicate they were available to meet up somewhere nearby. (p. 503)

Humphreys' description shows how location sharing can contribute to coordination as a social practice.[2] By communicating their location to a network of friends, Dodgeball users left open the opportunity for serendipitous encounters not likely possible if they communicated with one or two other people through text messages or voice calls. A Dodgeball message might tell one user that a friend is currently having a drink a block away. That knowledge may encourage the two people to contact each other and meet up at the location or somewhere nearby. That practice was common enough in Dodgeball that some of the people Humphreys (2007) interviewed saw coordination as the "correct" use of the service. These users expressed annoyance when friends checked in when they were not available to coordinate further social behavior.

While the design of contemporary applications that enable location sharing is different from Dodgeball, the occasional practice of sharing location with friends to coordinate behavior remains similar. A 2009 *TechCrunch* article describing Foursquare's launch stated that "Foursquare's primary function is to help you figure out where your friends are" (Kincaid, 2009: para. 2), and an iPhone commercial that highlighted Loopt featured a voiceover that said, "Staying in touch with friends can be tough. But if you have Loopt from the app store, you know what they're up to, where they are, and if they want to grab lunch." And coordination through these location-sharing applications can occur. In my research with Foursquare users (before the application moved check-ins to the Swarm application) (Frith, 2012a, 2014), I spoke with one individual who used the application primarily as a coordination tool with friends. He and his friends went out for drinks every weekend in a specific neighborhood in the Atlanta metro area. Often, they would not make plans and would instead head to a bar on a Friday or Saturday night, check in on Foursquare, and wait and see if other friends would respond to the check-in and show up. My findings were echoed in other research that detailed similar examples of people using check-ins as a way to let others know they were available to hang out (Licoppe, in press; Lindqvist, Cranshaw, Wiese, Hong, and Zimmerman, 2011).

As with many new communicative practices, a stable set of social norms likely does not yet govern how and why people share location on LBSNs and other social sites (Bertel, 2013b), and considering the lack of popularity of LBSNs, stable social norms may never arise. In addition, how and if people share location to coordinate will be impacted by the design of the applications. As mentioned earlier, Humphreys' Dodgeball research showed that some users were annoyed when people used the service for reasons other than coordination. Foursquare and Facebook, on the other hand, are more diverse applications. People can share location for a variety of reasons, and it is likely that such diversity complicates whether people actually use their location information to coordinate behavior (Frith, 2014). Almost every Foursquare user I spoke with told me their check-ins often did not necessarily mean they wanted to meet up and coordinate behavior, and Bertel (2013a) found the same in his exploration of why Danish youth share location on Facebook. Sociologist Christian Licoppe's (in press) interviews with French users of LBSNs revealed similar though not identical results. Licoppe's study showed that the "check-in is also a 'weaker' or looser form of invitation than more traditional ones, for it entails less obligations on the part of the recipient" (n.p.). In other words, seeing someone checked in nearby did not function as a traditional invitation to meet up. Instead, check-ins worked as a general "I am here" broadcast that people could either acknowledge or ignore with few social repercussions.

As explained earlier, check-in-based applications are different from location-tracking applications like Apple's Find My Friends, the now-defunct Google Latitude, and Glympse. While less research exists on how people coordinate through location tracking, different practices likely arise as a result of the different design approach. Glympse is an interesting example because it is designed with coordination as its sole purpose. With Glympse, users send friends a "glympse" as a URL through an email or text message, and whoever receives the link can then track the person's location in real time. The "glympse" then expires after a predetermined time, typically 15 to 30 minutes. Glympse does not feature other elements such as social networking or gaming, and the application represents what Tang and colleagues (2010) call "purpose driven" location sharing designed with one goal: to let other people track friends' movement as a way to coordinate behavior. Applications like Glympse are not nearly as popular as check-ins on Facebook, but they are a reminder that different models of location sharing will likely have different impacts on coordination practices.

Constructing identity through location

While people can use location-sharing applications to coordinate behavior, social location sharing is often not primarily a coordinative practice. In his description of the majority of research on location sharing, Licoppe (in press) argued that researchers tend to take a "perspective which can be described as informational, cognitive, and psychological: location checks are understood as actions making available information with the meanings and motives of an individual actor, the location checker, as the main focus of such research" (n.p.). This research tends to view the location shared as information that can either be used or ignored by people who have access to a friend's location. Instead, sharing location is a social negotiation among multiple actors.

Research focusing on social network sites (SNS) can help shed light on why location sharing involves a negotiation amongst multiple people. One of the most popular lines of SNS research concerns the presentation of self (boyd and Ellison, 2008; Hogan, 2010; Marwick and boyd, 2010), a concept drawn from Erving Goffman's (1959) influential sociological work on face-to-face interaction. Goffman argued that people constantly perform roles for multiple audiences. They dress a certain way to construct a certain identity on a Friday night and a different way on a Sunday morning. They use different language at dinner with their parents than they do at dinner with their friends. In Goffman's terms, social life consists of a series of performances. Interactions on SNS are no different. People put thought into the self they present to others on social sites (Turkle, 2010). They spend hours crafting profiles, pick flattering profile pictures, and write status updates meant to present themselves in a certain way. The choices they make show how communication is always a negotiation. People do not choose the information they display in isolation; they craft the self they want to display in relation to the people who will see their profile.

Research on LBSNs shows that the same occurs with location sharing (de Souza e Silva and Frith, 2012; Frith, 2014;

Humphreys, 2010). Many people share their location not to coordinate behavior but to present a specific identity to the members of their social network. For example, I interviewed a food enthusiast who would only check in to certain restaurants because he wanted to present that part of his identity to his friends. He secretly loved McDonald's but would never check in there because it did not fit with the foodie identity he had cultivated. Other people I interviewed also only checked in to interesting locations, and some participants told me they chose to share locations that "make themselves seem more interesting than they feel they truly are" (Frith, 2012a: 199). Bertel (2013b) also found that Danish Facebook users shared location more to show off to others than coordinate behavior. The cultivation of a certain identity through location led Cramer, Rost, and Holmquist (2011) to label location sharing as primarily a "performative act." People who have no intention of meeting up with others share their location anyway because they want their friends to know they went to a certain place. As Bertel's research suggests, this type of behavior is likely just as present, if not more so, on social sites like Facebook that people use to share location. Even before Facebook added its check-in feature, people posted status updates about concerts or sporting events they were attending as a way to highlight certain parts of their lives. Few people would assume these status updates were invitations to coordinate without inquiring further, and the same can be true of check-ins.

As the location features on sites like Facebook become more popular, location will possibly become an increasingly important part of how people construct identity on their SNS profiles, and Raz Schwartz and Germaine Halegoua (in press) introduced the concept of the "spatial self" to understand how people use location information as "online self-presentation based on the display of offline physical activities" (n.p.). The spatial self is a framework for examining how people use offline locations to construct online identity, and it can be particularly useful for future analyses of how larger SNS like Facebook and Instagram incorporate location into people's profiles. Facebook, for example, even features a location map that makes people's check-in history available to their social network by default. These maps become a new way to display one's mobility and ties to certain places over others. Where people go can say just as much about their identity as their list of favorite books, their political persuasion, or whom they interact with online. As more applications enable location tagging, people will continue to strategically highlight certain places as a way to present a certain self to their audience.

Sharing location and the future of public space

As with other social media, location-sharing applications have the potential to impact how people socialize with each other. That potential impact has raised an important question: how will these applications impact the future of public space? Public spaces are important parts of any city.[3] They are where people gather; they are where people are forced to confront others who are not like them. According to urban studies researcher Jane Jacobs (1961), this gathering of strangers is the defining characteristic of city life. Public spaces, defined loosely as anywhere that strangers congregate, are where people interact with those who are different from them and form a sense of self in relation to that difference (Sennett, 1977).

Mobile technology use can impact how people experience public space. As chapter 2 detailed, critics feared the Walkman would allow people to bring private experience out into public space (du Gay et al., 1997). Similar criticisms were expressed about the mobile phone (de Gournay, 2002). When people adopt a new form of mobile media, new concerns arise about how people use media to exert control over their experience of the public. The criticisms of location-sharing applications are slightly different from those of earlier mobile media, but they ultimately focus on the same issue of control (de Souza e Silva and Frith, 2012).

To examine the criticisms, it is first necessary to understand that the public spaces of the physical world are not the only publics in which people interact with and learn from others. Online sites like Facebook are now a new kind of networked public (boyd, 2007). In her description of interactions in networked publics, danah boyd (2007) wrote that "what makes these ... practices significant for consideration is that they take place in public: Friends are publicly articulated, profiles are publicly viewed, and comments are publicly visible" (p. 124). However, the online publics of SNS differ from the public of city life; on SNS people have more control over the public with which they interact. They cultivate their social network and play a role in creating their public, in contrast to a coffee shop or a city street in which the public is filled with strangers not of one's choosing. Consequently, the networked publics of SNS tend to be more homogeneous than the public life of the city.

One of the fears expressed about location-sharing applications is that they bring the worst of the self-sorting of online spaces (for example, the ability to interact only with one's network in networked publics) into the streets of the city (Frith, 2012b; Gordon and de Souza e Silva, 2011). As with other applications discussed in this book, LBSNs and SNS that include location sharing contribute to the creation of hybrid spaces. They merge physical location with social, digital information. People are able to map friends and sort through and filter the information they access about their surrounding space (Gordon and de Souza e Silva, 2011). The criticism of the self-sorting enabled by these applications was expressed eloquently by Alice Crawford (2007), who argued that services like Dodgeball encourage people to find "sameness in a sea of otherness and [connect] like with like – or the friend of like with like" (p. 89). Humphreys' (2010) work with Dodgeball users partially supported Crawford's argument and found that some people she interviewed used the service to seek out similarity: "Dodgeball informants did meet new people when using the service, the kinds of people they met were friends of friends and tended to be similar to themselves in terms of demographics such as age and education" (p. 776).

The question remains, however, as to how much of an impact these applications will have on the future of public space. While Crawford's criticisms are valid, people sought sameness long before they began sharing their location through mobile phones. In fact, a meta-analysis of literature on homophily, defined as "the principle that a contact between similar people occurs at a higher rate than among dissimilar people" (McPherson, Smith-Lovin, and Cook, 2001: 416), found more than 100 different ways people seek out similarity in their social lives, ranging from church groups to dining habits (McPherson et al., 2001). Consequently, while it is true that some location-sharing practices demonstrate "a desire to engage with an other that fits within the self's pre-established frame of otherness" (Farman, 2012: 73), this desire is not caused by location-sharing applications (Sutko and de Souza e Silva, 2011). People have long sought out others who are like them. The simple act of choosing one coffee shop over another often represents a decision to go where similar people congregate.

In addition, Crawford's (2007) criticism of mobile social software was made in the mid- to late-2000s at a point at which location sharing was near the peak of its hype phase. Gordon and de Souza e Silva (2011) also warned about self-sorting and location sharing when it seemed like Foursquare, Loopt, and other LBSNs would achieve mainstream status. That never happened. Most LBSNs failed, Foursquare split into two applications as a way to de-emphasize location sharing, and what happened instead was that large sites like Facebook and Instagram incorporated location as one of many ways people can share information with their social network. The future of location sharing will likely come as just one part of larger social networking applications, and at least in the near future, there is little to suggest that location sharing will become ubiquitous enough to have the kind of negative impact on public space feared by Crawford.

As a final point, even people who do share location are not necessarily only using the information to seek out people they already know. Nancy Baym (2010), in her book on relationships in the digital age, discusses the many different ways people connect with strangers online. These connections do not occur frequently, but they can lead to lasting relationships. The same is true of location sharing, and some location-based services focus more on connecting strangers than connecting friends. Possibly the two most popular examples are the location-based dating applications Grindr and Tinder.[4] Grindr was released in 2009 and targeted gay and bisexual males. The application's popularity has grown, and there are now more than 4 million users around the world ("Grindr | learn more," 2014). Grindr's interface relies heavily on location and displays other men's profiles in a grid that sorts the men based on how close they are to the user. The application is designed specifically for social discovery rather than for the strengthening of existing connections that is implicitly built into the LBSNs discussed earlier (Quiroz, 2013). Grindr encourages users to make connections with people they do not already know.

The dating application Tinder was not released until 2012, but it quickly gained attention and won TechCrunch's "Best New Startup of 2013" award (TechCrunch, 2014). Tinder allows users to swipe through the profiles of nearby people interested in making "matches" through the application (similar to Lovegety), and the startup's CEO claims the application has already been responsible for 1 billion matches (Ha, 2014). The application gained notoriety during the 2013 Winter Olympics when athletes began using it to find nearby matches in the Olympic village. The *USA Today* newspaper even ran a story claiming that "The biggest winner at the Winter Olympics is Tinder" (J. Anderson, 2014). The location-based dating landscape is filled with competitors, but Tinder now seems to be taking the lead in how different groups use location to connect.

Grindr, Tinder, and other location-based dating applications show how people can use location to find new people rather than simply connect with friends. Even on applications that focus more on reinforcing existing networks, in certain cases people can use the applications to meet new people. I end this chapter with an example from my Foursquare research.

In the summer of 2010, one of my interview participants – Dwayne – relocated to a suburb of Atlanta. Dwayne had been using Foursquare extensively before his move, and he decided to see if he could contact people through Foursquare because he did not know anyone in his new city. To do that, he began friend requesting people who checked in frequently to the gym he went to every day. On June 20, 2011, a woman named Elaine accepted his request and he asked her if she wanted to be Facebook friends as well so they could chat about the area. She accepted and they began conversing through Facebook and following each other's check-ins on Foursquare. On July 18, 2011, he saw they had both checked in to the gym, and they met in person for the first time. They immediately hit it off and had their first date on July 23. They were still together as of February, 2014.[5]

Dwayne and Elaine's story shows how people can meet strangers through location sharing. While Dwayne's connection with Elaine and many of the connections facilitated by dating applications like Tinder and Grindr likely represented a desire to seek out similarity, this type of behavior is certainly not caused by location-sharing applications. Most of the people individuals date, most of the people they are close to, share much in common with them. People go to certain coffee shops to engage with certain groups, attend events to find like-minded others, and create Internet dating profiles to search for matches. They often seek out sameness in the sea of otherness, but Dwayne and Elaine's example shows the ways in which social networking, combined with physical location, can lead to new relationships and impact how people meet others in contemporary hybrid spaces. Critics feared the Walkman and the mobile phone would contribute to a death of public sociability. However, public life remained alive and well, and it will likely stay alive and well as people share their location and map their social networks through various location-based services.

Conclusion

This chapter examined the phenomenon of social location sharing. A few services in the late 1990s and early 2000s, including Lovegety and Dodgeball, focused on using mobile technology to connect people in physical space. Later mobile applications, including Loopt, Brightkite, Latitude, Gowalla, and Foursquare, built on the goals of Lovegety and Dodgeball and took advantage of the capabilities of more technologically advanced mobile phones. These applications are called location-based social networks (LBSNs), and they encouraged people to create social networks and then share their location with friends.

This chapter examined social location sharing by first discussing the history of commercial LBSNs. LBSNs have struggled to reach a mainstream audience, and even the most popular LBSN – Foursquare – removed the social location sharing from its main application and created a separate Swarm application. The failure of most LBSNs and Foursquare's recent fissure suggest that location sharing may never fully take off in stand-alone location-based services. What is instead happening is that individuals are incorporating location sharing into various social sites, including Facebook and Instagram.

While location sharing has increasingly become one type of information among many shared on larger social network sites, earlier research on LBSNs is still relevant for understanding how and why people share location. As explained throughout this chapter, the sharing of location information provides new opportunities for people to coordinate social behavior. They can use location as a way to position themselves relationally to others, and that positioning can become a relatively new way to communicate and coordinate with friends. However, many people share their location with little intention of meeting up with others. Instead, they broadcast location as a performative act to present an identity to their social network, creating in effect a "spatial self" on sites like Facebook (Schwartz and Halegoua, in press).

The chapter concluded by addressing concerns about how

location-sharing applications may impact the future of public space. Alice Crawford (2007) argued that location-sharing services like Dodgeball may cause people to seek out homophily and avoid the difference present in the public spaces of the city. Her claims were partially supported by Humphreys' (2007, 2010) work with Dodgeball users; however, people tend to seek out sameness whether they are using location-sharing applications or not (Sutko and de Souza e Silva, 2011). In addition, location sharing has still not reached the mainstream and has likely not had the effect feared by Crawford.

The lack of mainstream adoption and the failure of most LBSNs does not mean location sharing as a social practice is not important. Survey research from the PEW Internet and American Life project showed that 30 percent of all social media users in the US share location on various sites (Zickuhr, 2013), and the act of sharing one's location or viewing someone else's location contributes to the formation of hybrid space and links offline activity to online identity. As argued in the introduction, locative media show how the separation of the digital and physical does not work analytically in today's world. Location sharing is a prime example of why that is true. When people share their location on Facebook or tag photos with location on Instagram, they share a piece of digital information about the physical world. They actively choose a place important enough to share with friends, and they partially build their online identity through their offline mobility. The digital and physical in this case are merged into a form of hybrid information, showing why it is important to recognize the social shifts with the adoption of smartphones as locative media. Of course, the social sharing of location information does more than impact how people use place to construct identity and coordinate with others; it also raises significant social privacy concerns, a topic covered in the second half of chapter 8.

6

Writing and Archiving Space

This past winter I was with my family on vacation in Venice, Florida, and decided to use my smartphone to find a restaurant. I pulled up a list of nearby places on Yelp. Once I had the list, I started reading what people had written about the restaurants. Some of these texts were basic reviews, but other people shared more personal experiences, such as a post from a man who wrote about taking his wife to their 30th wedding anniversary at a nearby Italian restaurant. Without the location-based services to find information about these restaurants, I would have never read those reviews or learned about that man's anniversary. The restaurant I chose was hidden on a quiet back street, a few blocks from Venice's main street. I would have never found the restaurant without my smartphone.

In the situation above, my experience of that city as a place was influenced by location-based digital information, a point that is key to the concept of hybrid space discussed in earlier chapters (de Souza e Silva, 2006). Hybrid spaces are physical spaces merged with digital information, and the two affect each other. The location-based texts described in the previous paragraph are one of the prominent informational layers of contemporary hybrid spaces. Through geotagging – defined as adding locational metadata to content – and other methods, people are able to produce digital content that is attached to locations. This content may affect how others experience a place and could signal a shift in who can create the informational layer of a place (Frith, in press). As architect Malcolm McCullough (2008) argued, the ability to write the "durable" layer of information that tells the story of a place has often been reserved for those in power. The powerful create monuments, the "official" narratives of the history of a place (Lefebvre, 1991). The city government creates the road signs, the business owners "write" space through their store fronts. Exceptions exist – for example, graffiti as a creative act – but most people are consumers of spatial information rather than producers. Smartphones as locative media alone do not change centuries-old power dynamics, but this chapter explores different ways people use location-based services to compose the information that becomes a part of their hybrid spaces.

This chapter also analyzes a different, more personal form of location-based composition: the use of locative media as a way for people to archive their past through location. Various location-based services, ranging from check-in applications like Facebook to route-tracking applications like MyTracks, enable people to use location as a way to remember their lives (Ozkul and Gauntlett, 2013). As discussed later, the use of location as a form of digital memory fits within the larger trend towards digital archiving mentioned in chapter 4 (Garde-Hansen, Hoskins, and Reading, 2009). The second half of this chapter focuses on memory practices, examining how smartphones as locative media can show the intimate relationship between memory and place.

Social media can make it difficult to draw a clear line between how people compose content for others and how they use media to store their past. A diary, for the most part, was a private media form people used to record their memories. Facebook has become a sort of twenty-first-century diary (Good, 2013), but it is also a social network site. People archive their moods as status updates and experiences as check-ins and photo albums, all in full view of members of their network. The same occurs on applications that focus specifically on location. Consequently, while this chapter is divided into two sections – one on location-based composition and one on location-based memory – the line between the two is not clear. Many of the forms of mobile composition examined below also create personal archives of people's mobility, and the mobile memory practices analyzed often involve social components. Both location-based composition and memory are worth examining in detail because they show how the digital and physical become intertwined through the use of location-based services; the digital compositions become spatial markers; the archived locations become digital traces of physical places. Both location-based composition and memory can make place into a physical/digital hybrid that is experienced differently through the interface of the smartphone, so the two areas covered in this chapter fit well with the larger trends traced throughout this book.

Mobile composition: Layering stories, reviews, and tips

Long before smartphones and app stores, philosopher Michel de Certeau (1988) wrote that "stories are becoming private and sink into the secluded places in neighborhoods, families, or individuals" (p. 108). A few locative media art projects, such as Urban Tapestries and Rider Spoke, sought to bring those stories back to the surface through explorations of location-based composition. Urban Tapestries was created in 2002 by the art collective Proboscis and enabled people to "embed social knowledge into the new wireless landscape of the city" by providing a platform people could use to geotag experiences of place that were then shared with others ("Urban Tapestries," 2005: para. 2). People who participated in the project came together to "write" central London in new ways, contributing geotagged personal experiences other participants could access through their mobile devices.

Blast Theory's Rider Spoke was another locative media art project that explored the potential of geotagged composition. Rider Spoke gave participants a specialized mobile device and a bicycle and told them to go to a "hiding place" in the city and answer a personal question chosen by the artists. The answer was recorded as a location-based audio track, and other participants received alerts when they were near someone else's contribution.

As the artists described, "The recordings that people make are only available in this context: player to player, alone, in the place where they were recorded" ("Rider Spoke," 2013: para. 6).

The types of location-based composition explored in these two projects were later incorporated into many commercial location-based services such as Foursquare, Yelp, and Socialight (Frith, in press). Most of these applications do not focus on personal, intimate stories like Urban Tapestries and Rider Spoke, but they do encourage people to contribute to the layer of digital information that can influence how other people "read" a place, and chapter 4 described people who use location-based services like Yelp to find nearby restaurants rather than planning beforehand. Location-based composition is what, in part, makes that flexible alignment possible. Another example is the location-based service Socialight that lets people attach "sticky notes" to locations. In their study of Socialight, Lee Humphreys and Tony Liao (2011) noted that

> One common way for Socialight participants to use the service was to tag locations they tend to frequent such as coffee shops, parks, and bars. These sticky notes became a means of communicating characteristics of various locations. For example, one participant, Nathan, used Socialight as a way to communicate with friends about places he likes in New York City. Most of his friends on Socialight are not from New York, so Nathan conceptualized Socialight as a personal travel guide. (p. 412)

Humphreys and Liao's interviews with Socialight users showed how the texts people "attached" to place impacted how others experienced the place. To put it differently, these location-based texts impacted what is called the "legibility" of places. Legibility refers to how places reveal themselves to people (Montgomery, 1998), and the "relevance of legibility lies primarily in the way that digital technologies can render the everyday world legible in new ways" by "making the invisible visible" (Dourish and Bell, 2011: 193, 195). The Socialight user described above made the "invisible visible" by using his smartphone as locative media to craft a networked, location-based travel guide for visitors to New

York City. He was able to share his experiences with other users who traveled to the places he wrote about, and what would previously have been personal, private experiences instead become attached to the locations and impact other visitors' behavior. The Socialight user in effect "writes" space through his location-based posts and other people can then "read" and perform the space differently.

The ability to access these geotagged messages as a way to "read" and "write" one's surrounding space relates to a point stressed throughout this book: the use of locative media can shift how people understand the relationship between mobile media and place. Mobile media scholar Jason Farman (2013), in a discussion of mobile storytelling projects, wrote that

> what mobile media storytelling projects demonstrate ... is that someone can be staring at a mobile device and be more deeply connected to the space and to others in that space than people might perceive. Storytelling with mobile media takes the stories of a place and attaches them to that place, offering an almost infinite number of stories that can be layered on to a single site. (p. 6)

The layering of spatial texts is what can make these forms of location-based composition such an important part of contemporary hybrid spaces. Reading about someone's positive experience of a place can impact how people view that place; the smartphone interface can become a screen through which people view a representation of their surroundings (Dourish and Bell, 2011; Frith, 2012b), and what they see through that screen can impact what Adriana de Souza e Silva and I (2012, 2013) called the "presentation of location." To develop the concept, we drew from Erving Goffman's (1959) work on the presentation of self, discussed in chapter 5, to suggest how location-based composition can impact the impressions people form about the identity of locations. We argued that the new ways in which people create location-based texts can reveal the dynamic nature of locations because impressions can change as more people compose the digital identity of a place.

Locations rarely, if ever, have identities separate from other social factors. Even famous sites are shaped in great part by the fact that people travel long distances to visit them (MacCannell, 1999). The identities of bars, restaurants, and other commercial locations are also shaped by the people who visit. So the presentation of location is not necessarily something new; people have always played a role in constructing a place's identity, and as Massey's concept of a "progressive sense of place" suggests, places do not have static identities that cannot change. What shifts is how this construction increasingly takes place through digital information, specifically the mobile composition enabled by locative media.

Review sites like Yelp are an example of how important this location-based layer of user-generated texts can be. Yelp is both a website and a popular location-based service, and people use it to find places and read others' reviews and experiences of those places. How important is this digital layer to the presentation of location? In some cases, very important. Many restaurants in the United States have stickers in their windows saying "people love us on Yelp." Establishments have threatened to sue individuals over bad Yelp reviews (Mayer, 2013), and Yelp has been accused of extorting businesses by threatening to emphasize bad reviews over good ones (Zara, 2013). Some Yelp users even bring "Yelp reviewer" cards to restaurants and then get special treatment because the establishments are aware of the power the reviewers hold over the way their location is presented (Worstall, 2013). The role Yelp reviewers play in constructing how these locations are perceived relates to the power dynamics mentioned in the introduction. Before location-based services like Yelp became popular, a select few food critics reviewed restaurants publicly and left the durable trace of their dining experience in the form of published reviews. Now that power has moved partially into the hands of everyday patrons who can post to Yelp and other similar mobile applications like Urban Spoon or Google Places. The durable informational layer of the place becomes more polyvocal, and while the act of leaving a simple review or tip at a location on Yelp may seem mundane, a study by Harvard Business School professor Michael Luca (2011) found that an improvement in Yelp reviews can result in a 5–9 percent increase in a restaurant's revenue. As more people rely on locative media to navigate physical space, these location-based texts and ratings will become an increasingly important part of contemporary public space.

While reviews and tips may represent the bulk of location-based texts, people can also use locative media to explore more unique forms of mobile composition (Farman, 2013). For example, an Italian restaurant in my city features a Yelp review from a man who wrote about how he and his wife went there on their first date almost 20 years ago. The review is only one of many, but it offers a glimpse into someone else's story of a place. Another example of how people can use commercial location-based services as a platform to encourage others to "see" differently comes from an amateur photographer I interviewed for my Foursquare research (Frith, 2012a). The man used Foursquare to leave photography tips at popular locations in Cincinnati, Ohio. When people checked in to those locations, they saw his tips explaining the best angles to photograph the site, the times of day the lighting is best, and the ideal camera settings to capture different features of the place. His tips encouraged other users to read the place differently, to understand the place as something to be photographed and captured in certain ways. These kinds of location-based texts might not be the primary use of location-based services like Yelp or Foodspotting, but they do show how people can use location to share their experiences of place with others who, in turn, may incorporate those experiences into their own experience of or behavior in that place.

Many examples of mobile composition, ranging from reviews on Yelp or Google Places to stories on Socialight, are textual; however, people can also impact how places are read in other ways, including sharing geotagged pictures through applications such as Instagram or sharing their mobility through applications like Facebook. The next section looks more closely at how non-textual forms of mobile composition may further impact the legibility of contemporary public spaces.

The non-textual writing of space
One of the prominent ways people can both read and write space is through geotagged image sharing with mobile applications such as Instagram or Flickr (Hjorth and Pink, 2014). Instagram is a photo-sharing application created in 2010 and acquired by Facebook in 2012. The application is most famous for allowing people to apply filters to photos and then share them with their Instagram network. Instagram users can also geotag their photos and upload them with the longitude and latitude at which they were taken (Hochman and Manovich, 2013). Before 2012, however, geotagging on Instagram was not a particularly useful feature because people could not easily map others' photos. Then Instagram introduced the "photo map" feature that lets people create public maps of pictures they uploaded. These photo maps can be a detailed, highly specific way of viewing the city. Other users can "'drill down' using this interactive map and study the various places a user has taken photographs, down to street-level specificity. The results are displayed on a hyper-local level so that users can see photos that were taken in different parts of the same street" (Schwartz and Halegoua, in press, n.p.).

Photo maps on Instagram as well as other photo-sharing sites like Flickr and Picassa rely on the types of technological location awareness discussed in chapter 2, but another way people write the city relies on hashtags. Hashtags are popular on Instagram, Twitter, and other social media, and they are a method people use to organize data. People who tweet or share pictures about the same topic, event, or place can hashtag their posts so they show up in searches. Hashtags are not a direct form of location awareness, but they can serve a similar function. They enable people attending an event to include the event's hashtag in their Instagram picture or tweets. Or users may create a hashtag describing a popular place, such as the #nationalmall hashtag. The hashtag then becomes a collection of images people have shared about that place, and anyone searching from the Instagram mobile application can access these pictures appended with the hashtagged location. Just like with actual location tagging, hashtags are also available on other photo applications, and the physical location becomes the metadata people use to organize their photos.

Texts and images are both explicit ways of writing space, but people can also affect how others read space simply by sharing their location. Humphreys (2010) found that Dodgeball users were more likely to go to certain places if they saw other Dodgeball users went there as well. My work with LBSN users revealed similar findings: multiple people told me that seeing friends had checked in to a place made them more likely to go there (Frith, 2012a). For example, a woman I interviewed found a small market in her New York neighborhood because she saw that two of her friends frequently checked in there. She decided to go to the market because she knew those friends lived in another part of the city and had to travel out of their way to visit that particular place. The same situation could easily occur through someone sharing geotagged or hashtagged photos on Instagram or check-ins on Facebook. The simple act of being at a place and sharing it on social media can affect how others read their surrounding space by highlighting a specific location as one worth visiting (Sutko and de Souza e Silva, 2011).

The sharing of location can also write the city through mobility; de Certeau (1988) argued that the act of walking writes the city in new ways. Walkers reveal routes, paths, and trajectories, and play an active role in constructing the city as a lived space. The location features of applications like Facebook have the potential to allow for a more networked form of writing the city through mobility. Frequent Facebook users may check in multiple times on an active day. By publishing those check-ins in a linear fashion, they may create links among places in other people's minds as a possible path to follow (de Souza e Silva and Frith, 2012). Adriana de Souza e Silva and I (2013) called these collections of check-ins "spatial trajectories," and the networked nature of services like Facebook allows people to share these check-ins as a way of writing space for others. These "spatial trajectories" can affect the presentation of location explained in the previous section, and as discussed below, they also open up new opportunities for remembering the past through location.

Mobile remembering: Composing memories in place

Memories are often closely tied to place. People remember where they were when significant events happened. They remember the rooms they lived in as children. Nations build monuments to establish places as sites of collective memory (Lefebvre, 1991). To return to the quote from philosopher Edward Casey (1996) mentioned in chapter 2, "to know is first of all to know the place one is in" (p. 18). The same can be said of memories. To remember is often to remember the place one was in.

Memories are also tied to external objects. People have photo albums that visualize their past (Sontag, 2001), shoeboxes filled with letters from exes, and various mementos that remind them of past experiences. Increasingly people also mediate their memories through digital media. Facebook has become a twenty-first-century digital scrapbook (Good, 2013), seen notably in the Facebook "10 year anniversary" videos that created a linear montage of users' Facebook activity. The same is true of other forms of social media: digital photo sites become the public, networked photo album (Hand, 2012); personal blogs become networked diaries (Miller and Shepherd, 2004). As chapter 4 showed, people increasingly offload their memories to digital media.

Location-based services merge the spatial nature of memory with networked forms of digital memory, enabling new opportunities for people to use mobile media to remember their lives through location. These mobile applications can become part of the "new memory ecology" that is increasingly shaped by social media people use to both remember and share their experiences

(Garde-Hansen et al., 2009). To provide more detail on the different practices of location-based memory, this section briefly describes how three types of location-based services explore individual issues of memory: location-sharing applications, route-tracking applications, and location-based mobile games.

The first type consists of applications like Facebook and Instagram that enable people to tag posts with location information. Tagging posts with location information means the posts can then be returned to as a way of tying a past moment to a particular place. Memory was already shown to be a primary reason people used Foursquare before the application moved check-ins to Swarm (Ozkul and Gauntlett, 2013), and the same can be expected in future analyses of how people return to their location data on other location-sharing applications. Facebook's check-in map, for example, provides people with a map of their check-ins as a way to visualize and archive their past through location. The Instagram photo map discussed above becomes a location-based pictorial archive of the locations people felt were worth photographing and sharing. Ultimately, as Didem Ozkul and David Gauntlett (2013) wrote, location-based services can "be used to keep a record, a biography or a diary. People go back to their photos, mobile Facebook status updates, or Foursquare check-ins to remember those places and recall their memories" (p. 121).

Another category of location-based services that shows links between place and memory is that of "route-tracking" applications. Most applications that feature route tracking are fitness applications such as MyTracks and Ghost Tracker Pro. These applications feature maps that trace the exact route users take, allowing people to record their hikes or runs. The "tracks" get stored on the phone and on the Web, and they become a new way in which people archive their mobility. Whereas check-ins enable people to record specific places they visit, route-tracking applications focus more on the journey than the destination, creating an archived visual representation of one's physical mobility rather than a map of specific places one highlights through check-ins.

The final application mentioned here is the mobile game Fog of World. When people open Fog of World on an iPhone, they see a map covered in fog. The fog dissipates when they physically travel to a different place and uncover new parts of the map. The application encourages people to go to new places and view their mobility as a game because each new route reveals more of the map and adds to their total mobility archive. The focus on the relationship between memory and place is explicit in the application's tagline – "Remember everywhere you have been in your whole life journey!" – and, as I argued with Jason Kalin (in press), "As the app removes the fog floating on the user's map, it also removes the fog of memory by showing where the user has been and still needs to go. Memory of places and places of memory thus become active forces for future exploration" (n.p.). Location-based games, and even location-sharing applications like Facebook, can turn physical space into something to be collected and remembered and acted upon. Each new place people visit adds a piece to the spatial memory archive they compose through location, and these archives can then influence later behavior. Someone may return to a location archived through Facebook, retrace a route they recorded on MyTracks, or visit a new place not yet revealed on Fog of World or a place not yet experienced on other mobile games like Plague, Inc. The practice of archiving through location can then become a new performance of location at a later date.

Checking in, route tracking, and mobile gaming show the complex relationship among mobile media, place, and memory. They also show how memory practices have been impacted by the rise of social media. Media scholar Andrew Hoskins (2009) introduced the term "digital network memory" to explain how social media enable memory practices that are increasingly public. He views digital network memory "as something created when needed, driven by the connectivities of digital technologies and media, and inextricably forged through and constitutive of digital social networks" (p. 92). As he points out, the act of mediating memories is increasingly tied to how people construct their identities in front of their social networks. Facebook is a prime example. People store their memories through photo albums, check-ins, and updates, but much of the memory-making process becomes public so that people write themselves into being in front of their audience (boyd, 2007). The Facebook photo album is simultaneously a personal collection of memories and an identity crafted in public view of one's Facebook network.

The location-based services discussed above also represent forms of digital network memory, and they show why it is not easy to draw a clear line between location-based composition and location-based memory practices. People who check in primarily as a way to create an archive of their locations still "write" space for anyone in their network who sees the location being shared. Fog of World allows people to compete over the total physical area they uncover on their map, so one person who archives a new location may encourage another player to do the same. Route-tracking applications like MyTracks and Ghost Runner have sharing features that let people publish the maps they create through their mobility. These maps can be a form of writing space that is then read by others who may choose to follow the path traced on the map.

These location-based services all provide techniques people can use to both remember and share place and mobility. The examples provided in this section are only a small subset of location-based services that help people remember through location. Google Maps stores previously visited locations, and mobile storytelling projects provide ways for people to both archive and share their stories of place (Farman, 2013). Location-based memory is only one part of the larger push towards personal digital archiving, but it will likely become an increasingly important part as people use smartphones to write and record space in new ways.

Conclusion

Much of the content people access through location-based services is created by other users. People read reviews on Yelp and Urban Spoon, see photo maps on Instagram, and view people's shared locations on Facebook. As this chapter has shown, these types of content are examples of people "writing" space. People contribute location-based information that becomes an important informational layer in contemporary hybrid spaces, and that information can affect how others experience a place.

This chapter discussed how different types of content, including location-based texts, images, and shared locations, can all be considered forms of "writing" space for others to read. Mundane activities such as sharing a geotagged picture on Instagram or writing a review on Yelp can encourage other people to go to that place. These are all examples of how the digital layer of hybrid spaces can affect the perceived identity of locations. Consequently, many places are becoming hybrid spaces. Mobile media users are walking hybrid spaces that create hybrid spaces wherever they go. Being in, living in hybrid spaces can impact how users perform space – altering behaviors, experiences, and identities.

The second half of the chapter transitioned to a focus on location-based memory. As discussed, people can use a variety of location-based services to archive their experiences through location. These mobile applications show the close ties among memory, place, and media, and they are an increasingly important part of "digital network memory" (Hoskins, 2009). The examples detailed – including Foursquare, Facebook, MyTracks, and Fog of World – also show how social media have impacted individual memory practices. Many of the ways people use location-based services to remember also involve the production of content that can impact how others view a place. Importantly, these practices are not exclusive to the applications discussed above. If these applications all failed, other applications would take their place and people would find new ways to build spatial memory archives through location-based services.

Practices of mobile composition and mobile memory participate in the broader trend in digital culture of living private lives in public. Whereas de Certeau argued that stories are becoming private and that secrets are hidden in places, locative media show how private spatial stories can become public and how places not only accrete but also secrete secrets. Both location-based composition and location-based memory also participate in the shift signaled by the growth of locative media: the merging of the physical and digital. Writing reviews on Yelp and tags on Socialight can impact how places are experienced and who can participate in their social construction. Even a MyTracks tracked run can merge the physical with digital, altering the meaning of movement by making the spatial experience of the offline something to be collected and shared as a piece of digital data. The act of accessing another person's experiences of a place through location-based reviews or narratives can alter how a space is understood and experienced, and the decision to add one location rather than another to a spatial archive can change the personal meaning of a place. Just as navigation applications impact how people negotiate mobility and location-sharing applications turn physical locations into part of one's online life, the practices of location-based composition and memory show how contemporary places are being affected by the adoption of smartphones as locative media.

7

Market Forces and the Shaping of Location-based Services

"Success" is an interesting word when discussing technology startups. I teach computer science students who design mobile applications, and for them, getting an application approved by the Apple store qualifies as a huge success. Many other mobile applications are side projects, and any money they make is a bonus. And yet, when tech sources talk about the success or failure of mobile applications, they often set a remarkably high bar. Foursquare is an interesting example. As of April, 2014, Foursquare had over 45 million users, 50 million unique visitors to the website's search page, and the company had raised over $100 million in various rounds of funding. Compared to 99 percent of the applications available in the Apple and Google app stores, Foursquare has been a huge success. However, none of those numbers, none of that comparative success, has stopped private research firms from making bold predictions like "Foursquare WILL fail by the end of 2013" ("Privco's top 10 2013 predictions," 2013).

Foursquare has run into the same problem that many other social media startups face: how can they make money from the data they collect? Other popular mobile applications never had to address this question because they were acquired by larger companies. Instagram was bought by Facebook for $1 billion (Raice and Ante, 2013); Waze was bought by Google for $1.1 billion (Efrati and Rubin, 2013). Foursquare reportedly turned down acquisition offers from Facebook and Yahoo (Ante, 2010), instead seeking out investors to fund the company's growth. The need to chase further investment has led to multiple attempts to promote Foursquare as an advertising platform and increasingly position the application as a major player in the growing "local search" market. In May, 2014, Foursquare even split into two separate applications: Foursquare and Swarm. The Foursquare application focuses on local search and competes with applications like Yelp and Urban Spoon; the Swarm application features the check-ins that initially won Foursquare so much attention. This chapter details how financial pressures helped lead to that split.

Foursquare's struggle to monetize the application is not a unique one. For as interesting as location-based services are from a sociological standpoint, it is important to remember that most of these applications are businesses. Unlike locative media artists, developers of location-based services are primarily interested in creating a service that can eventually make money. This chapter uses Foursquare as a case study to examine the role that market forces play in shaping location-based services. The goal is not to provide a full history of the application, but rather to show how important venture-capital funding can be for startup companies. A key focus of this chapter concerns analyzing how the design of the application has changed as the developers have experimented with different ways to make money from location data and how those changes eventually led to the splitting-off of the check-in function into the separate Swarm application. The next chapter focuses on the privacy concerns of location-based services, but by detailing just how valuable location data can be through my case study of Foursquare, the following sections begin raising the privacy questions that are explored in more detail later.

Tracing Foursquare

Foursquare's roots trace back to the late 1990s when Foursquare co-creator Dennis Crowley began building an online city guide at dodgeball.com.[1] He then joined New York University's ITP graduate program in 2002 and, with Alex Rainert, designed Dodgeball as his thesis project. While Dodgeball remained a relatively small service, Google acquired it in May, 2005, for an undisclosed sum, and Crowley became a Google employee. Crowley hoped Google would continue to develop Dodgeball, but he left the company in 2007 and publicly expressed his frustration:

> It's no real secret that Google wasn't supporting dodgeball the way we expected. The whole experience was incredibly frustrating for us – especially as we couldn't convince them that dodgeball was worth engineering resources, leaving us to watch as other startups got to innovate in the mobile + social space. (Crowley, 2007)

After Crowley left Google, he worked for the startup Area/Code, which is where he met Naveen Selvadurai who worked at another startup in a nearby office. The two men shared an interest in location-based services, but they did not finalize plans to build their own application until Google finally shut down Dodgeball for good in January, 2009 (which was not coincidentally one month before Google released Latitude). Crowley and Selvadurai immediately began working on the application that would become Foursquare, and two months later, Foursquare debuted at the South by Southwest (SxSW) festival.

Crowley's experience with Dodgeball influenced the later design of Foursquare, which began as an updated version of Dodgeball that took advantage of the new technical capabilities of smartphones. Whereas Dodgeball relied on text messaging to share location, Foursquare used location-awareness and the mobile Internet. Unlike most other LBSNs at the time, such as Loopt and Brightkite, Foursquare also featured gaming elements such as points, badges, and mayorships. The combination of gaming and social networking led to some confusion of terminology in early articles about the application, with some people labeling Foursquare a location-based social network (LBSN) and others calling it a mobile game. Regardless, Foursquare was an instant hit at SxSW and was later grouped with Twitter as one of the most successful launches in the festival's history (Marwick, 2013). Within a week of its release, Foursquare had already been featured on a *New York Times* blog (Wortham, 2009), the influential social media site *Mashable* (Van Grove, 2009), and the popular tech source *PC Magazine* (Monson, 2009).

Foursquare entered an already crowded market. Loopt, Brightkite, Whrrl, and Gowalla had all already been operational for over a year; Google's Latitude was released a month before Foursquare. Foursquare's main competitor was likely Gowalla, in part because Gowalla was a similar application that also featured check-ins and mobile gaming. However, Foursquare grew at a much faster rate than Gowalla, hitting 1 million users by April, 2010, while Gowalla failed to hit the 1 million user mark until 2011. Foursquare then passed the 5 million user mark by December, 2010, and at one point showed a faster growth rate than Twitter (Yarow, 2010).

While Foursquare grew much faster than its competition, some people remained skeptical, arguing that Foursquare would fail as soon as a larger site like Facebook added location features (Gaudin, 2010). In August, 2010, Facebook added a location layer with its Facebook Places application, which emulated Foursquare's check-in model. Facebook's entry into the location-sharing market led to articles like CNN's "Facebook steals Foursquare's location crown" (Cashmore, 2010) and predictions that Facebook Places would quickly kill Foursquare (Carlson, 2010). However, Foursquare continued to add users, passing 10 million users by June, 2011.

And Foursquare continued to grow even as other services like Twitter and Instagram also added location sharing. Foursquare now has users all over the world and a staff that has grown from a handful of people to over 160. As I discuss later in this chapter, Foursquare users have produced a huge data set of location information that other applications, such as Instagram, use to power their location services. That data set has been crucial to the development of Foursquare's Explore feature, which works as a recommendation-based spatial search engine that people can use to find nearby places. Yet Foursquare is still an application with an uncertain future that has never fully surpassed niche status. For all of its success, the percentage of smartphone users who report using the application to check-in has actually decreased (Zickuhr, 2013), and many people doubt that check-in applications will ever become mainstream (Bertel, 2013b). Foursquare's developers recognized that problem and began moving away from the check-ins and gaming on which the application was originally focused, but only after experimenting with various monetization strategies. The move away from check-ins and gaming eventually led to a split in which the check-ins that were the focus of the earlier version of Foursquare were removed completely and a separate check-in application called Swarm was created. The next section details the monetization and market pressures Foursquare has faced, and the chapter concludes by discussing how these pressures have affected the design and focus of the application, eventually contributing to the creation of Swarm.

The importance of venture capital

Why are so many people skeptical about Foursquare's future? The reason lies in the long history of Internet startups that developed a user base but failed to make money. The late 1990s dot-com bubble was the most famous example. Online companies raised large amounts of money and had soaring stock prices despite never establishing stable revenue streams. The dot-com bubble peaked in early 2000 with the NASDAQ hitting a then record high, but it burst later that year and a host of now infamous eCommerce sites like Pets.com and Boo.com crashed completely. In hindsight, the problem with the dot-com bubble seems fairly simple: A significant number of Internet startups were spending large amounts of money while earning little.

The stock market did not completely stop speculating on Internet companies' potential after the dot-com bubble burst. Other famous Internet companies, such as Amazon and Twitter, have market valuations that far outstrip their reported profits (Bensinger and Calia, 2013). Instagram reported $2.7 million in losses in 2012 (Thomas, 2012), but that did not stop Facebook from acquiring the application for $1 billion. Snapchat, another mobile startup, turned down a $3 billion acquisition offer from Facebook despite not having a consistent revenue stream (Lee, 2013). What makes these companies so valuable is not the money they make; it is the money people believe they can make in the future (Lee, 2013). Foursquare's projected value also relied mostly on speculation, focusing more on the potential value of its data rather than actual revenue.

As a startup, Foursquare had to raise money to keep operating and growing. One of the first rounds of funding came in September, 2009, six months after the application debuted at SxSWi. The first funding round was a relatively small $1.35 million led by Union Square Ventures (Siegler, 2009). At the time, Foursquare had fewer than 50,000 users but had already begun to explore monetization strategies, which I discuss in more detail in the next section. Foursquare then raised $20 million in June, 2010, amid rumors Facebook and Yahoo were interested in acquiring the company (Ante, 2010). Before the second round of funding became official, some sources had speculated on whether or not Foursquare would choose to sell (Parr, 2010), but Crowley came out publicly against the idea: "The best shot we have to build all the things we want to do is hinged on staying independent" (Ante, 2010: para. 9). Crowley's desire to stay independent is likely related to the negative experience he had when Google acquired Dodgeball. That decision, while it does have the benefit of giving the developers more power over the future of the application, raises the need to seek out future funding and experiment with new ways to make money.

Foursquare continued to grow after its second round of funding, and in June, 2011, the company added $50 million of funding, headlined by the venture capital firm Andreessen Horowitz. This major round of funding valued Foursquare as a $600 million company (Carlson, 2011), up from the $120 million valuation that accompanied the previous round. At the time of the cash inflow, investors were still banking on Foursquare's potential. The company still had little revenue and was spending more money than it was making, which, according to the popular blog *TechCrunch* (Lacy, 2011), scared away some investors.

The future became more uncertain after the significant cash inflow from the third round of funding, and people in the tech press began arguing that Foursquare had no clear path towards monetization (Sweeney, 2012). Foursquare attempted another round of funding in 2012, but investors apparently balked at the asking price. The company was reportedly spending $2 million a month while only showing $2 million in revenue for all of 2012 (Sweeney, 2012). The lack of revenue did not stop venture-capital firm Spark Capital Partners LLC from purchasing $30 million of Foursquare stock at a price that valued Foursquare's worth at $760 million (Ante, 2012), but experts later said that valuation was significantly too high (Flamm, 2013). Foursquare was then unable to raise funding at a high enough valuation, and instead turned to a $41 million round of convertible debt rather than equity funding (Crowley, 2013). Raising debt rather than funding had the advantage of avoiding a potentially embarrassing situation in which the company's valuation dropped from previous rounds, but it also increased "the pressure on the company to prove it has a real business" (Ingram, 2013: para. 1).

After the round of debt funding, Foursquare was then able to raise another $35 million in funding from a variety of venture-capital firms. The round, completed in December, 2013, valued the company at slightly over $600 million (Swisher, 2013). Foursquare then received $15 million in funding from Microsoft in February, 2014. The Microsoft funding was more of a partnership between the two companies than a traditional inflow of outside capital (Panzarino, 2014). The partnership includes a licensing agreement that allows Microsoft to use Foursquare's location data to improve the Bing search engine and Windows 8 phones. That deal also shows where Foursquare's true value lies: its local search data rather than its check-in function. While the application began as a check-in-based social network, it has positioned itself as a local search engine and harnessed the power of its location data to provide relevant local results, and in retrospect, the Microsoft partnership looks like a harbinger of the eventual splitting-off of non-search-related functions into the Swarm application. Later in the chapter, I provide a more detailed description of how Foursquare's location data may contribute to future monetization and explain the fissure of the application in more detail.

Monetizing location

Foursquare's first attempt to establish revenue was likely its "specials" campaign. Businesses could offer specials that Foursquare users saw when they pulled up a list of nearby locations. The locations were highlighted on the list, and the specials consisted of messages like "free appetizer for your first check-in" or "the Foursquare mayor gets a free espresso." Merchants could choose when and how to offer these location-based advertisements, and in interviews I performed with Foursquare users, I found that some people began using the application specifically to access specials (Frith, 2012a).

The specials feature also enabled Foursquare to build corporate partnerships. The first prominent nationwide Foursquare special was with Chili's, an American chain restaurant (Gallo, 2011). Any Foursquare user who checked in to Chili's received a free order of chips and salsa. Other notable partnerships included Starbucks (1$ off a Frapuccino for the Foursquare mayor) and entertainment companies like The History Channel and Bravo that created a branded set of badges Foursquare users could earn (Gallo, 2011). The most high-profile partnership Foursquare formed was likely with the American credit card company American Express. Beginning in 2011, American Express users were offered discounts at places for checking in to Foursquare. Users linked their American Express account to their Foursquare account, went to a place with a special, checked in, used their card, and then received the discount on their credit card statement. To some observers, the partnership represented a potentially valuable revenue stream for Foursquare, and a *New*

York Times article claimed that this type of partnership "may bring Foursquare and other location-based services further into the mainstream" (Wortham, 2011: para. 5). Other sources saw the partnership as a model for the future of location-based advertising (Vazquez, 2011). While partnerships gained a great deal of early attention, Foursquare has increasingly moved away from that model to focus more on spatial search.

Foursquare also developed its Merchant Platform, which lets businesses "claim" their location and then access data about who checks in, when people are most likely to check in, how many people are repeat customers, and so on. The Merchant Platform provides businesses with a significant data source to understand their customers' (at least their customers who use Foursquare) behaviors and was the focus of one of the first books about using Foursquare for advertising. In the book *The Power of Foursquare*, Carmine Gallo (2011) discussed how Foursquare's Merchant Platform can help businesses harness the power of location data to connect with customers. The book is similar to many other social media marketing books that overstate the benefits of social media for making money, but some investors agreed with Gallo about the potential of the Merchant Platform, and the $50 million round of funding that Foursquare received was meant to help the company build the platform (Carlson, 2011). As of March, 2014, over 1.6 million companies used the Merchant Platform ("About Foursquare," 2014), but just as with other monetization attempts, it is unclear how much money Foursquare makes from this service. In addition, the decision to remove check-ins from the main Foursquare application means that the Merchant Platform now has a more uncertain future than ever.

Location-based advertising and the Merchant Platform are both visible parts of Foursquare's plans to establish revenue streams. A less visible, though more important, part of that plan comes from the huge amount of data Foursquare has collected. Ambitiously, Dennis Crowley has responded to Foursquare critics by claiming that the application is "becoming the location layer of the Internet" (McDermott, 2013: para. 15). A *TechCrunch* article written by entrepreneur Jonathan Barouch (2013) explains how this works. First of all, Foursquare has collected a huge amount of location data. People have checked in over 5 billion times, and importantly, most of the locations people check in to are created by users. The huge database of location names and addresses has become an essential part of the location-based application ecosystem. To date, over "40,000 developers use Foursquare location data via their API" (Barouch, 2013: para. 3). Many of the services that use Foursquare's API to retrieve location information are small, but not all. Popular applications such as Instagram, Uber, and Foodspotting all rely on Foursquare's API to provide their users with location information. Even Twitter's Vine service uses Foursquare to power its location service.[2] As Barouch argues, "Any destabilization in Foursquare or its developer tools would fundamentally affect the stability of the mobile web" (para. 1). Barouch also points out that Foursquare's reach extends far beyond its 40 million users: "by adding together the unique users of the popular applications that Foursquare powers, you would find that its data touches several hundred million users" (para. 5). People who use a variety of location-based services interact with Foursquare data without even knowing it.

Crowley's goal to turn Foursquare into the "location layer of the Internet" is certainly ambitious, though Foursquare still does not charge developers for access to its API. However, the API may signal a way the application can make itself indispensable and eventually turn its location information into revenue. Barouch argued that, with the reach of Foursquare's location database, it is now in Apple and Google's best interest to work with Foursquare to make sure it succeeds:

> Foursquare remaining healthy and maintaining an open API is critically important to Apple given the reliance on Foursquare of so many popular iOS applications.
>
> And while Google has an excellent Places database of its own, it too has an interest in ensuring Foursquare's longevity.

> Those same app developers that fill up Apple's App Store charts are also pumping out applications on Google Play that rely on Foursquare data. (para. 6)

The applications built on Foursquare's API rely on Foursquare's continued success. If Foursquare fails, many location-based services would have to find a new location source, and it can be a "significant engineering effort to migrate off Foursquare's data" to a different source (Barouch, 2013: para. 8). Only the future will tell if Foursquare can turn its API into revenue, but the application continues to focus on building its location layer, and the company received $15 million from Microsoft primarily because Microsoft wants access to Foursquare's location data. The focus on the "location layer" became even more pronounced when Foursquare moved check-ins and gaming from the main application to the Swarm application, focusing solely on local discovery through location information in the Foursquare application. As Crowley (2013) argued, the ultimate goal of the application is to become "the platform that all other companies use to power location in their applications" (para. 6).

From social network to search

Foursquare began fairly modestly, and there was no talk of becoming the "location layer of the Internet" when the application was released in 2009. Instead, Foursquare focused on two main things: mobile gaming and social location sharing. Both these elements helped establish the popularity of the application. Before check-ins were moved to Swarm, people had checked in billions of times on Foursquare, and many companies had sponsored badges people could earn through their check-ins.

Despite its growing popularity, Foursquare still faced the perception that it was a niche service that had limited utility and limited opportunities to produce revenue. Consequently, the application began to move away from check-ins and mobile gaming. In 2012, Crowley stated that "If anything we might have de-emphasized the check-in a little bit" (Taylor, 2012a: para. 4). Then, in 2013, Crowley did a round of media interviews, arguing that Foursquare is much more than a social network and mobile game: "Foursquare is much more than mayorships and badges. It's a perception issue. We've definitely been phasing a lot of that stuff out" (Bilton, 2013: para. 3). What Crowley points out in this statement is what anyone who regularly used the application had already realized: Foursquare was moving away from check-ins and gaming and moving towards emphasizing spatial search and location recommendations.

The move away from social networking and gaming began in early 2011 when Foursquare introduced the Explore feature. Explore is a spatial search and recommendation engine based on an algorithm that draws from the large data set of Foursquare check-ins to recommend new locations based on where "people like you" go (Moore, 2011). Consequently, Explore might tell users they will like a nearby bar because two of their friends have already been there. Or it could tell users a nearby restaurant is popular with people who go to a restaurant they already frequent. The use of friends' check-ins to make personalized recommendations can be particularly useful because, as Foursquare engineers explained in a presentation on Explore, over 60 percent of people's check-ins are to locations where someone in their Foursquare social circle has already been (Moore, 2011).

The search feature slowly became more and more prominent in the application's interface. An August, 2013, update to the Windows 8 version of Foursquare even went so far as to remove the social feed that told users what their friends are doing (Carr, 2013a). Foursquare also developed "Pilgrim" which passively tracks users' locations and then gives them push recommendations about nearby places. So if Foursquare uses Wi-Fi location to detect that a user had visited four Mexican restaurants, the applications would send a push notification when the user was near another Mexican restaurant whether they had checked in or not. Then in May, 2014, Foursquare made the announcement that analysts following Foursquare's evolution had expected: the application was moving away from check-ins and gaming once and for all. In a blog post, the company announced the creation of a new application called Swarm (Foursquare, 2014). The original Foursquare application retained the logo and the search and recommendation functions, while all of the check-ins, gaming elements, and social feeds moved to Swarm. Most importantly, by keeping the search function in the Foursquare application, users did not have to download a new application to continue using Explore and other recommendation features. They did have to go to the app store and download Swarm if they wanted to continue checking-in and sharing their location with friends. The creation of Swarm was a tacit acknowledgment that the future of the application lay in local search, not location sharing.

Foursquare's shift in design is notable even among social media startups. The application has moved from one thing (a social network/mobile game) to another (a local search engine), "deemphasizing check-ins and highlighting its tools and information to search for and discover great places" (Carr, 2013b: para. 22). The changes cannot be divorced from the monetization pressures detailed above. Foursquare gained users by focusing on gaming and social networking, but it was difficult to make money from check-ins. The company established corporate partnerships, created location-based advertising opportunities, and built its Merchant Platform, but it still faced serious questions about its future. The focus on local search and the decision to eliminate check-ins from the main application put Foursquare in the same class as other local search applications like Yelp, which has a valuation of over $1 billion (Taylor, 2012b). Tellingly, in a blog post describing the company's 2013 round of debt funding, months before the creation of Swarm, Crowley never mentioned gaming or check-ins. He instead compared Foursquare to Google, claiming that Foursquare will revolutionize spatial search in much the same way that Google impacted online search: "we think of Foursquare as having the ability to give people superpowers for exploring the real world" (Crowley, 2013: para. 5).

So what can this brief history of Foursquare reveal about location-based services in general? Most importantly, Foursquare's story is a reminder that the location-based services discussed in this book are businesses. Their goal is to make money, and if the mobile applications do not make money, most will likely fail. Also, the majority of these applications are free, meaning companies do not make money from downloads. As the famous saying goes, "When something online is free, you're not the customer, you're the product." The data produced by people using location-based services like Foursquare are used to power advertising schemes, merchant platforms, and search algorithms. Even established, multibillion-dollar companies like Facebook and Twitter have struggled to find consistent revenue streams, and the current market for location-based services is just as uncertain.

Building on that point, one of the most revealing aspects of this case study of Foursquare is the vital importance of data in the location-based services market. Foursquare's projected value comes from the data it has collected from users, and competing applications like Yelp and Urban Spoon will also focus on data collection as a prime way to increase revenue. Foursquare's example also reveals the crucial role various APIs play in the mobile ecosystem. The people who hold the data potentially hold the power because their APIs supply other applications with information used to shape their products. If Foursquare were to cut off its API, the mobile ecosystem would suffer. Other location-based services are likely also interested in collecting data and creating APIs that allow access to that data. The importance of user data to power algorithms and APIs is an important point relevant to many of the most popular location-based services.

Finally, Foursquare's example shows that monetization pressures can shape the design of existing and future location-based services. Foursquare was successful as a mobile game and social network. It built a user base where Brightkite, Whrrl, Loopt, Gowalla, and others failed. But it still moved away from gaming and social networking in part because of an unclear path to future profit, eventually resulting in the creation of the stand-alone Swarm application. Other applications that struggle with monetization may also alter design goals as a way to improve their applications' chances of success. Consequently, Foursquare serves as an important reminder that money will play a significant role in shaping the design of the next generation of location-based services.

Conclusion

Most location-based services are businesses. The people who develop them want to make money, whether through revenue or through acquisition by a larger company. This chapter used Foursquare as a case study to examine the business side of location-based services. Foursquare has faced many of the same struggles as other social media startups. Even as the application added users and gained popularity, it struggled to find consistent revenue streams. To examine the business side of Foursquare, this chapter provided background on the application's funding history, its attempts at establishing viable revenue, the splitting-off of the check-in function to the Swarm application, and Foursquare's shift in design to establish itself as the "location layer of the Internet."

The goal was to do more than give background on one application; instead, this chapter shows the vital role that market forces can play in shaping present and future location-based services. Foursquare began as one thing – a social network/ mobile game – and became another: a spatial search engine with one of the mobile Internet's most important location APIs. Other location-based services face similar market pressures, and Yelp, for example, has sought to expand by adding check-in functions and creating new features for businesses as a way to establish revenue. Other applications that use location information, such as Instagram, chose to be purchased by larger sites like Facebook. Foursquare is only one example of the struggles that location-based services face, but its struggle is not unique. Future location-based services will also need to find ways to make money, and as this chapter discussed, it can be difficult for mobile applications to establish consistent revenue streams. That struggle can result in shifts in design and explorations of how to use people's location data for new marketing schemes and new search algorithms. Consequently, huge databases of location information, such as the information collected by Foursquare, also raise questions about the role people's personal data plays in the monetization of location-based services, a topic explored in the next chapter.

8

The Negotiation of Locational Privacy

I have been studying locative media for half a decade now, and the majority of questions I get about my work concern privacy. If I give a talk on mobile mapping, an audience member almost always asks what happens to our location data. If I talk to family or friends about social location sharing, I get questions asking why anyone would let other people know their location. These are good questions, and the answers are more complicated than they might seem.

One of the problems with discussing privacy is the difficulty in nailing down just what is meant by the term. Most people have experienced situations in which they felt their privacy was violated. But it can be difficult to provide a workable definition of what they mean by privacy. Privacy, after all, is not an objective entity; how privacy is understood greatly depends on culture. For example, Paul Dourish and Genevieve Bell (2011) discussed how in some Asian countries it can be perfectly acceptable for a waiter to ask a female customer about her menstrual cycle, a question that would quickly get a Western waiter fired. In addition, privacy is always about more than just keeping information to oneself, regardless of culture. If people post a status update or share their location on Facebook, they want other people to see what they share. That does not mean they do not care about privacy. They do not want *everyone* to see what they share. They want to be able to control who accesses their information and how far their information travels.

Consequently, this chapter draws from social media researcher danah boyd's (2011) work to conceptualize privacy as "the control over a social situation" (para. 1). This general definition posits that when people are able to exert agency over what they share and with whom they share it, they are able to maintain their privacy (boyd, 2011; Dourish and Bell, 2011; Solove, 2008). Importantly, privacy within this framework is not simply about the control of information, and the complex privacy settings on a site like Facebook do not ensure people maintain their privacy. Instead, people must be able to understand the different contexts in which their information is shared (boyd, 2011), which is true whether the information is the location people share with their mobile network carrier or a check-in on Facebook.

Importantly, a network carrier's ability to access and store location information is different from that of friends who can see the locations people share on Instagram or Facebook. For that reason, this chapter divides locational privacy issues into two groups: *institutional* and *social* privacy (Raynes-Goldie, 2010).[1] The next section discusses institutional locational privacy, which addresses how governments and companies collect location data. The chapter then moves on to social locational privacy by focusing on how people negotiate location sharing with other individuals. While it is outside the scope of this chapter to pro- vide a comprehensive account of how governments, companies, and individuals collect location information, the goal of this chapter is to shed light on current practices and raise concerns about how the increasing reliance on location information may have consequences for locational privacy.

Institutional locational privacy

Mobile phones were location aware long before they began incorporating GPS or Wi-Fi positioning. The United States implemented the E911 system in the 1990s so that emergency services could locate mobile phones within a roughly 100m radius. With landlines, the phone number one called from was tied to a physical location; with mobile phones, that was no longer the case until E911 implemented the tower triangulation methods discussed in chapter 3. While E911 was supposed to only allow emergency services to access people's location, privacy advocates feared that law-enforcement agencies would also use the system to obtain location information, and one critic argued that with E911 "your phone has become an ankle bracelet" (Oakes, 1998: para. 15).

In addition, people's location information was valuable from a commercial perspective long before they began using mobile phones. In 1971, Jonathan Robbins founded Claritas, a company that maps the demographics and purchasing preferences of zip codes for marketers. My zip code tells me that where I live features a mix of low- to middle-income people with a median income of $44,400. Services like Claritas (now called PRIZM) currently segment populations down to the zip code +4 level, meaning they can paint a fairly accurate picture of small areas for marketers. As geographer Mark Monmonier (2002) argued, services like Claritas raised privacy concerns about using location to tailor advertising.

With the adoption of smartphones, concerns about E911 or zip code marketing seem rather tame. People now walk around with devices that can be located to within 3m, and a huge amount of location information is stored in multiple databases on a daily basis. The warnings about the implementation of E911, however, seem prescient in the wake of revelations about the data-collection practices of the National Security Agency (NSA) in the United States. Concerns about advertising tailored to location also seem to predict the kinds of location-based advertising seen with smartphones, which make zip code segmenting seem innocuous in comparison. To examine these concerns, the next section focuses on governmental surveillance before moving on to how commercial entities collect location data.

Governments, law enforcement, and location data

Pretty much anyone who has watched a twenty-first-century spy movie knows not to use a mobile phone if he or she is trying to avoid being tracked. In fact, even if the phone is turned on but not used to make a call or access mobile data, network carriers log the location of the mobile phone using triangulation methods discussed in chapter 3. The logging of location information is not in itself negative: mobile telephony will not work if carriers do not know which cell towers a phone is near at any given time. However, the major concern about cell carriers' collection of location data comes from the storage rather than the collection. The American Civil Liberties Union (ACLU) revealed that all US carriers retain users' cell tower locations for one year, and some carriers retained the information for more than three years (ACLU, 2011). As the ACLU argues, carriers do not need to store data for such extended periods, and doing so raises important concerns about how data is handled and the ways in which it is used.

Security researcher Christopher Soghoian showed that US law-enforcement agencies often request carriers' location records, and these requests are rarely, if ever, rejected (Zetter, 2009). In some cases, law-enforcement agencies do not even need warrants to access someone's cell location history, and in the US, it is nearly impossible to get a detailed picture of law-enforcement practices regarding location data:

> The government's location tracking policies should be clear, uniform, and protective of privacy, but instead are in a state of chaos, with agencies in different towns following different rules – or in some cases, having no rules at all. (ACLU, 2012: para. 10)

Some court cases, such as a 2–1 ruling in the US 5th Circuit Court of Appeals, found that law enforcement does not need a warrant to access location data because the data are merely "business records" and use of "phones, moreover, is entirely voluntary" (Crump, 2013: para. 6). That court ruling was echoed by a New York court that found warrants are not required to access a cell phone's location history because "cell phone users who fail to turn off their cell phones do not exhibit an expectation of privacy" (quoted in Soghoian, 2013: para. 1).

Law enforcement's tracking of location data is by no means confined to the US. In 2011, *The Daily Mail* reported that London law enforcement purchased state-of-the-art tracking software for accessing phone location (Daily Mail, 2011). In that same year, German police in the city of Dresden illegally collected the cell location information of thousands of protestors at an anti-neo-Nazi rally (Benzow, 2011). More recently, the Ukrainian government used cell location data to send the following text message to anyone in the vicinity of an anti-government street protest: "Dear subscriber, you are registered as a participant in a mass disturbance" (Murphy, 2014).

Location data also played a role in Edward Snowden's revelations about the data collection practices of the US's National Security Agency (NSA). Snowden's documents revealed the agency had enacted a top-secret pilot program during 2010–11 to "test the collection of bulk data about the location of Americans' cellphones" (Savage, 2013: para. 1). The head of the NSA claimed location data was never collected through the program, and he claimed that the program is not currently operational. However, one of the documents published by journalist Glenn Greenwald showed that the NSA "is currently collecting the telephone records of millions of U.S. customers of Verizon, one of America's largest telecoms providers" (Greenwald, 2013: para. 1). According to Greenwald's report, if individuals either own a phone on the Verizon network or called someone on that network, their locational metadata is likely now part of an NSA database. At this point, it is still difficult to determine the full extent of the NSA's collection of location data, but the Verizon example shows the agency has already built a huge database of people's locations, and questions remain about the extent to which other nations engage in similar practices.

Despite the many relevant concerns about institutional locational privacy, the collection of location data can serve a social good. Mass analysis of mobile phone location data has already been used in various Big Data approaches to battle disease in Africa (Talbot, 2013), pinpoint traffic congestion in the United States (Brehm, 2012), and trace the effects of disasters in Haiti (Bengtsson, Lu, Thorson, Garfield, and Schreeb, 2011). There is also an argument to be made that security agencies' access to location data has helped thwart attacks and fight crime, and as the E911 example mentioned earlier shows, cell-phone location data is useful during times of personal emergency. So individual locational privacy concerns should be balanced by the acknowledgment that mobile location data can be used for social good. That does not mean, however, that concerns about individual locational privacy should be explained away by claims to a greater good. As this section has briefly discussed, most people have no idea how their data is collected and used, and as Mayer-Schönberger and Cukier (2013) explain in their more general discussion of Big Data approaches, it is important for people to understand how their data is collected and how it will be analyzed. Benefits do exist, but so do drawbacks, and people should be made more aware of the potential for both.

Commercial use of location data

Online advertising has become more advanced as companies have figured out new ways to collect personal data (Turow, 2012). Google personalizes advertisements based on previous browsing history; large marketing companies combine cookie information from multiple sites to tailor advertisements. Location-based advertising (LBA) is the logical progression, and marketers were hyping the benefits of using location as far back as the early 2000s (Kolmel and Alexakis, 2002).

At the most basic level, LBA comes in two forms – push and pull (Unni and Harmon, 2007). With the push form, consumers sign up – or do not sign up in some cases – for location-based advertisements and they then receive a text-message advertisement when they walk close enough to a certain type of store (Greenfield, 2006). Companies have been slow to roll out this form of advertising, likely in part because people reacted negatively to earlier text-message-based advertising (Maneesoonthorn and Fortin, 2006). Research also shows that people have significant privacy concerns about push LBA: in a study of 153 individuals, Ramaprasad Unni and Robert Harmon (2007) found that "privacy concerns are high, and perceived benefits and value of LBA are low" (para. 1).

The other method of LBA is the pull method. With the pull method, people log in to an application, look up information about their surroundings, and receive a special coupon or advertisement for something nearby. The Foursquare "specials" discussed in the previous chapter are an example of pull LBA. The difference between push and pull is that with pull LBA people have to open a specific application. Research suggests that the pull method will likely be more successful because it raises fewer privacy concerns (Unni and Harmon, 2007).

Regardless of the methods companies adopt in the future, marketing research shows that more and more companies are using LBA campaigns. Research by eMarketer showed that 36 percent of mobile marketing campaigns used LBA in 2012, an increase from 17 percent in 2011 (eMarketer, 2013). Research group Nielsen found that 33 percent of consumers thought LBA was useful (Moth, 2012). Though LBA expenditures still pale in comparison to traditional advertising and online advertising, they represent a growing segment of many advertising budgets.

While LBA is still relatively new, mobile marketing is already at a point at which the data collection practices of smartphones and mobile applications are just as unclear as data collection online. This uncertainty can be seen in a 2010 article published in the *Wall Street Journal* (Thurm and Kane, 2010). The article's authors tested 101 popular smartphone applications. Of those 101 applications, 47 transmitted the phone's location information. Many of the applications did so without any mention in their privacy policies about using location information, and some applications did not even have privacy policies. While some applications, such as the location-based services discussed throughout this book, have to access people's location to work properly, many other applications access location for no apparent reason besides advertising. For example, the privacy policy for the popular mobile game Angry Birds states that the application "may collect and process your location data to provide location related Services and advertisements" ("Rovio privacy policy," 2013: para. 15). Applications like Angry Birds do not need to access users' location to work properly; they collect location information to provide advertising, and an application developer told the *Wall Street Journal* that "ads targeted by location bring in two to five times as much money as untargeted ads" (Thurm and Kane, 2010: para. 42).

Mobile carriers have also explored ways to make money from the location data they collect, and in 2013 Verizon rolled out the "Precision Marketing Insights" program that captures: "information from the physical and digital worlds simultaneously to deliver unparalleled audience and location measurement, mobile marketing and predictive analytics based on what audiences actually do, where they actually go and what they actually like."[2] Verizon's description of the program states that it allows companies to "Isolate where consumer groups work and live, the traffic patterns of a target audience and demographic information about what groups visit particular locations." And Verizon is not the only carrier experimenting with using people's location data in aggregate form. Spanish telecom Telefonica has also begun to sell anonymized consumer location data as part of its "Big Data" push. A Telefonica spokesperson explained the value of the program with the following statement: "Retailers are quite good at measuring footfall inside their stores, but this data will tell them where people go once they are outside, as well as their age and gender" (BBC, 2012b: para. 7).

Carriers and mobile applications both collect location data; Google and Apple do as well. A study found that phones running Google's Android OS "collected [their] location every few seconds and transmitted the data to Google at least several times an hour" (Angwin and Valentino-Devries, 2011: para. 3). Apple also collects the anonymized location data of iPhone users. In 2011, security researchers Peter Warden and Alistair Allan found that people can even access a file on the iPhone that reveals "the latitude and longitude of the phone's recorded coordinates along with a timestamp, meaning that anyone who stole the phone or the computer could discover details about the owner's movements using a simple program" (Arthur, 2011: para. 2).[3] Apple's location tracking became more explicit with the iOS 7 update that added an opt-in "Frequent Locations" feature that tells the user the places they visit most frequently and uses the data to improve Apple Maps. While Frequent Locations is an opt-in feature, people's locations are still collected by Apple by default regardless of whether they turn on the feature.

The list of companies that collect people's location data is far more extensive than the few cases covered in this section. Chances are, if someone accesses a mobile application that uses location, her data is being stored on a server somewhere. Even if she uses applications that do not need location, her location is still likely to be stored on a server somewhere. Just as with the location data discussed in the previous section, there are potential social benefits to this data collection. Google and Apple collect location data to improve their traffic and Wi-Fi location features. For example, location data collection is what powers Google Maps' traffic features. Advertisers collect location data to provide relevant ads, which some consumers do want (Moth, 2012). So this data collection is not inherently negative. It does, however, raise important concerns, and the next section explains why all this matters.

Why institutional locational privacy matters

The data collection practices detailed in the previous two sections are often shrugged off with an all too common refrain: the "Nothing to Hide" argument. The argument has different variations, but it ultimately amounts to, "If I'm not doing anything wrong, who cares if the government or a company has access to my data?" As legal scholar Daniel Solove (2011) argued, the "Nothing to Hide" argument often dominates privacy debates but misses the complex nature of privacy. People all have things they do not want to be shared. They have curtains on their windows, passwords on their email, and doors to their rooms.

People also do not want to share their movements with everyone. I recently had a reminder of how revealing location information can be. The Dallas-Fort Worth area where I live has a toll system that takes pictures of cars' license plates and then mails a bill months later. When I received the bill, I was surprised by how much the recorded data revealed about my actions. The bill listed 14 times I had passed through tolls and included the exact location of the tolls, the date, and the time. Was I doing anything wrong when I passed through those tolls? No. But that does not mean I would want that bill to be shared with just anyone. I could have been traveling to an interview at a nearby university. I could have been consulting a divorce lawyer or attending a political protest. I could have been planning a surprise for my significant other. These examples serve as a reminder that, even if people are not doing anything illegal or immoral, it still makes sense to care about the types of data the government and companies collect about their location, especially in light of the growing number of security breaches at major companies. The example also shows why locational privacy is not a black or white issue. The toll collection does serve a basic social good: Dallas does not have toll booths that slow traffic because it captures cars' location through license plates or toll tags. The system is more convenient and faster even as it raises concerns about how people's locations are tracked every day.

To many people, the data collection discussed above will bring up the specter of George Orwell's *1984*. In fact, the Big Brother metaphor has shaped much of the discussion of corporate and governmental surveillance. However, Solove (2004) argues that the reliance on that metaphor to understand data collection obscures more than it reveals. Most people do not have their every move watched by law enforcement or various companies. Instead, Solove argues that institutional privacy is better understood using the metaphor of Franz Kafka's *The Trial*. In *The Trial*, the main character is arrested by a faceless bureaucracy and accused of a crime. He is not told what the crime is or what evidence exists against him. As Solove (2011) writes, "the problem is not inhibited behavior but rather a suffocating powerlessness and vulnerability created by the court system's use of personal data and its denial to the protagonist of any knowledge of or participation in the process" (para. 19).

Solove's adoption of the Kafkaesque metaphor puts corporate and governmental collection of location information in a new light. Even if people are not actively watched, their privacy is still impacted by the massive collection of information because they cannot find out what information different entities possess. In addition, even when location data is used for projects designed for social good, such as improving traffic flow or tracking disease, people should be made aware of who has access to their data and how it is being analyzed. Going back to boyd's (2011) definition of privacy, people have little control over the social situation in which their location information is collected. The process of doing research for this chapter put this into a stark light for me personally. I read everything I could find on the data collection practices of the NSA, law enforcement, and various companies, but I still do not have a clear idea of what location information is out there about me or who has access to that information. Privacy expert Joseph Turow's (2012) work on online privacy paints the same picture; people simply do not have a good way of knowing what their data profiles are. Location information is only one part of people's huge digital profiles, but it is becoming an increasingly significant part. Even if they have not been directly affected by this data collection, people should continue to be concerned about institutional locational privacy while also recognizing that this data can be used in positive ways to improve traffic and track disease. The balance between individual informational privacy and the social good is a pressing issue, and location data has become part of that debate and will continue to be so as governments ramp up data collection efforts and companies find new ways to profit from people's personal location data.

Social privacy

Research with Facebook users has shown that people tend to be more concerned with what Internet Studies researcher Katherine

Raynes-Goldie (2010) calls *social privacy* than what companies do with their data (boyd and Hargittai, 2010). Research I did with Foursquare users revealed similar findings (Frith, 2012a). The people I interviewed cared more about what other people could see about their check-ins than what Foursquare did with their location data. They shared location with friends, but they expressed concerns about how best to control what others could access.

As with other types of personal information, the location information that people share with others cannot be simply divided into either private or public. This point is addressed by danah boyd (2008) in her criticism of developers who view privacy in binary terms as either 0=private or 1=public. Privacy is far more complicated than that and involves the ability to understand the social situation in which one is sharing information. Most information is fine to share in certain situations with certain people and not acceptable to share in other situations. It is neither completely private nor completely public. Social locational privacy should be thought of in those terms as a negotiation of various social contexts. At certain times, in certain situations, people may want to share their location with members of their social network. That does not mean they want everyone to know their location, nor does it mean they do not care about their locational privacy.

However, adding location to social networking does mean people have to navigate an altered information landscape. They have to develop ways to share location information while maintaining a sense of privacy, just as they develop tactics for sharing other types of information on social sites such as Facebook. Research has shown that Facebook users create lists to control who can see their posts, use alias accounts to protect their identity, develop coded language that only makes sense to friends, and alter default privacy settings (boyd and Hargittai, 2010; Raynes-Goldie, 2010). As people fold location into the everyday information they share with others, they must adopt new strategies to protect their sense of privacy. To examine how they do so, the next section discusses existing research on social locational privacy.

Social locational privacy
Much of the research on locational privacy has examined location-sharing systems that are different from commercial mobile applications; however, these studies have reported interesting findings useful for understanding how people manage locational privacy concerns. Two examples are a study of parolees who had their location tracked by the state of California (Shklovski, Vertesi, Troshynski, and Dourish, 2009) and a study of children who had their location tracked by their parents (Boesen, Rode, and Mancini, 2010). In both these studies, the research participants developed tactics to control their location information. Parolees faced severe consequences if their location-tracking technology failed, so they changed their mobility patterns to make sure they were able to keep their GPS devices charged (Shklovski et al., 2009). More pertinently, teenagers who took part in the family-tracking study developed multiple ways to control the location information transmitted about them to their parents. The authors note that "Limitations in technology were exploited to make someone appear where they are supposed to be even if they are not, allowing kids to break the rules" (Boesen et al., 2010: 70). This finding relates to Dourish and Bell's (2011) more general description of "digital deception" as a privacy tactic, which argues that mobile systems must allow people to misrepresent their location as a way to exert control over the information they share.

Two other studies took a more quantitative approach to studying locational privacy. Lederer, Mankoff, and Dey (2003) conducted a survey asking people to imagine how they would respond to situations in which someone requested their location. They found that people's decision whether or not to share location was strongly influenced by their social situation and the identity of the person requesting the information. Sunny Consolvo and colleagues (2005) studied how 16 people felt about disclosing their location through an SMS service similar to Dodgeball. They found that 77 percent of the time their participants disclosed their location in fairly accurate terms (e.g., an address or a place name), but they also found that disclosure was greatly influenced by both who was doing the requesting and when the request occurred. Participants in these studies put conscious thought into choosing what information to share, which is an important point to remember when discussing social locational privacy.

As these studies suggest, the ways people approach locational privacy cannot be completely separated from the design of the applications they use. The children in the family-tracking study found limitations in the technology that they could exploit. Consolvo and colleagues' experimental location system was designed to give people control over what they shared; consequently, the two major location-sharing designs covered in chapter 5 – location tracking and check-ins – likely have some impact on how people manage their locational privacy. Take location-tracking applications as an example. Purposive location-tracking applications like Glympse rely on ephemerality as a privacy tactic. People choose when to have their location tracked, and the tracking ends when the predetermined time period expires. The ephemerality of the "glympse" gives people control over when they share their location and for how long. Google's Latitude and Apple's Find My Friends, on the other hand, represent a more passive location-tracking process that does not feature the same type of ephemerality. With these applications, people do not have to actively choose to share their location each time, which increases the chance they leave the application on without realizing it (Page and Kobsa, 2009).

The most popular model for social location sharing is the check-in model, and for the purposes of this section the word "check-in" is used liberally to include actual check-ins on LBSNs and Facebook, as well as voluntary location tagging in applications like Instagram. Check-in-based applications require people to actively choose when to share location with friends, and Cramer, Rost, and Holmquist (2011) argue that check-in systems mitigate "problematic issues such as privacy" (p. 9). To explain how, I turn to interviews I did with Foursquare users (Frith, 2012a). While my research focused on Foursquare before the check-ins moved to the Swarm application, many of the privacy tactics users developed likely apply to other location-sharing applications such as Facebook and Instagram.

The most obvious way the Foursquare users I interviewed protected their privacy was by limiting who was in their network. My participants also created "alias" accounts that did not reveal their identity, similarly to Raynes-Goldie's (2010) findings about Facebook users. These alias accounts allowed people to access Foursquare specials and earn badges without the risk of people they knew finding them through the application. Other tactics people developed were more specific to location-based social networks. My research participants would often only check in as they were leaving a place so they could broadcast a location without running the risk of someone stopping by. They would basically misrepresent their current location as a form of "digital deception" just like the teens in the family-tracking study. Multiple female users reported engaging in this tactic, and people can do the same thing by sharing location on Facebook or uploading geotagged pictures on Instagram only as they leave a place. Finally, my research participants also used different layers of location to protect their privacy by doing things like checking into their neighborhood or apartment building rather than their actual home address. Because so much of Foursquare and other applications' location tagging relies on user-generated location names, people can create "higher-level" locations that reveal less about their actual physical location. The ultimate point is that most people who use these location- sharing applications do take audience into account and do still care about their privacy. They develop a variety of tactics that shape the types of information they share.

The unintended consequences of location sharing
The Foursquare users I interviewed praised the control they had over their check-ins; however, unintended consequences did

occasionally occur. People told me stories about friends who said they were not going out who went out anyway and checked in on Foursquare. The friends seemingly forgot the person with whom they canceled plans was their Foursquare friend and could see their check-in. Other people shared their location frequently until something happened to remind them of the possible consequences. When people checked in to a location on Foursquare (now on Swarm), other Foursquare users at that location could see they were checked in and could see their Foursquare thumbnail photo. Occasionally, other Foursquare users would approach them and identify them by their thumbnail photo, and these situations made some of my participants uncomfortable about sharing location information so freely.

Here is where the complicated nature of locational privacy comes into play. Someone's location is rarely ever truly private. If someone goes to a cafe, other people at that cafe can see she is there. Even if the user is at home, she likely has a car in her driveway that suggests she is there. However, it still bothered some of my research participants when they were approached and identified through their location sharing. To best understand their discomfort, it helps to turn to sociologist Georg Simmel's (1950) framework of urban life (de Souza e Silva and Frith, 2012). Simmel argued that urban individuals are both public and anonymous at the same time. They constantly share the streets with strangers, but because of the sheer number of people, they are able to maintain their privacy by blending in (Lehtonen and Mänpää, 1997). When someone broadcasts their location through a location-based service, they sacrifice some of that anonymity and can be picked out of the crowd (Sutko and de Souza e Silva, 2011). Sociologist Christian Licoppe and Yoriko Inada (2009) detailed an example of this loss of anonymity in their research on the location-based mobile game Mogi, in which people share location with other players: at one point in the game, a male player told a female player that he could see her in physical space because she had shared her location information. She did not know who he was because he refused to share his physical location through the game. The female player felt uncomfortable and called on two other male players to help. Licoppe and Inada frame this as a power asymmetry because only one person could see the other's location on the mobile phone, and this example is a realistic approximation of what can occur when people share their location through various applications.

Two websites – PleaseRobMe and ICanStalkU – also explored the unintended consequences of location sharing. PleaseRobMe aggregated public tweets from people who shared their Foursquare check-ins on Twitter. Foursquare, just like Facebook, relied on a limited network approach. Only friends can see all of someone's check-ins. Twitter, by default, is a public social site. When people linked their Foursquare check-ins to Twitter, everyone could see the location being shared. Despite the title, the goal of PleaseRobMe was not to get people's houses robbed; the site's creators were instead concerned with "raising awareness about oversharing" by showing people they were publicly sharing their location with anyone interested enough to look. The site gained attention from major sources such as the *Guardian* (Halliday, 2010) and the *Toronto Star* (Song, 2010), and Foursquare's developers published a blog post addressing concerns raised by PleaseRobMe (Foursquare, 2010).[4]

Like PleaseRobMe, ICanStalkU's goal was "Raising awareness about inadvertent information sharing." ICanStalkU focused on people who shared geotagged photos on Twitter, often without realizing it. Many smartphones automatically embed pictures with locational metadata, so when someone shares one of these photos, anyone can access the photo's metadata to find the longitude and latitude at which it was taken. ICanStalkU emphasized this with a feature called "What are people *really* saying in their tweets" that took people's often innocuous photos and changed the text of the tweet to "I am currently nearby [location]." Both PleaseRobMe and ICanStalkU publicized information as a way to alert people to the consequences of location sharing, and they are a reminder that people may not always be fully cognizant of what they share on social media.

The final example mentioned here of the unintended consequences of location sharing is the short-lived mobile application GirlsAroundMe. GirlsAroundMe looked a lot like a standard location-sharing application. When people opened it, they saw a Google Map with their location. However, where GirlsAroundMe was different from Foursquare or Facebook was the button in the top-left corner that filled the map with the thumbnail pictures of women at nearby locations. GirlsAroundMe worked by drawing from the public Foursquare and Facebook APIs to display the locations of women who publicly shared their check-ins (Brownlee, 2012). To make matters worse, the application user could click on the thumbnail and go to the woman's Facebook profile to read more about her, see her pictures, and possibly see a list of her interests, depending on her privacy settings. Most of these women likely had no idea that their check-ins on Facebook and Foursquare were public, leading to the type of power asymmetry discussed in the earlier Mogi example. Once people began paying attention, Foursquare killed GirlsAroundMe's ability to access the Foursquare API, and Apple pulled the application from the iOS store (Brownlee, 2012). However, GirlsAroundMe is yet another example of the possible consequences of location sharing and exposed – not that it was the application developers' intention – the potentially gendered nature of locational privacy by showing that women may face a unique set of concerns when sharing their location.

Conclusion

This chapter examined locational privacy issues and drew from the work of Katherine Raynes-Goldie (2010) to divide privacy concerns into two sections: institutional and social privacy. Institutional privacy focuses on how governments and companies collect data. The chapter first examined the lack of a clear legal framework dictating when and how the government and law enforcement can access people's location data before moving on to the similar situation people face when trying to understand how companies handle location data. The collection of location data by large entities is not inherently bad, and location data has been used for projects that work for the social good. However, it is almost impossible to fully determine which entities have access to people's location information. So, drawing from Daniel Solove's privacy framework, the major concern about institutional locational privacy is that people have little control over how their information is collected or how it is used.

The chapter then moved on to social locational privacy concerns. People can now share location with their friends using a variety of location-based services. The addition of location to the other types of social information people share requires the development of new tactics for managing privacy, and those tactics are relevant whether discussing LBSNs or larger social sites like Facebook that enable people to share their location. The social privacy section concluded by examining three sites – PleaseRobMe, ICanStalkU, and GirlsAroundMe – that all show why people need to remain aware of the location information they share with others. Location can be a useful piece of information for navigating public space, keeping up with friends, and contributing spatial information. However, with the growth of location-based services, place and mobility has become a commodity of sorts, a piece of information transmitted to large entities and members of one's social network. The locational privacy concerns discussed in this chapter are one of the possible negative social impacts of the growth of hybrid spaces, and those concerns will only become more pressing as more and more people use smartphones as locative media.

Conclusion:
The Future of Locative Media

One of the challenges of writing a book like this is that mobile applications can change in between drafts of chapters. Two days after this book is published, Google could release an update that changes Google Maps; Instagram could redesign the photo map; Glympse could change its ephemerality model. That dynamism is why this book focuses on user practices rather than the specific design of applications. While mobile interfaces may change, the general reasons people use locative media – finding places, mapping friends, writing about places, archiving mobility – will survive in one form or another.

The dynamic nature of locative media can also make it difficult to write a chapter about the future. Many smarter people than me have made bold predictions about emerging media that ended up being wrong, and the future of smartphones as locative media could still head in many different directions. Consequently, rather than focus solely on theoretical predictions about the future of location-based services, this chapter covers three sections that examine the near-term impacts of the increasing adoption of locative media: (1) location-based services and the global South; (2) location-based services and digital inequality; and (3) the near future of locative media.

The first section examines the global South. This book has focused almost exclusively on fully industrialized nations, in part because of my own limitations as a researcher in the United States and in part because global South countries have only recently seen widespread smartphone adoption. To examine the future of smartphones as locative media in the global South, the next section discusses the impact of earlier mobile telephony, analyzes the smartphone as a "leapfrog" technology, and explains why location-based services will likely be developed in culturally specific ways. The chapter then moves on to a discussion of the future of inequality and locative media. This section focuses on more than simple demographic numbers (who owns smartphones and who does not) and instead discusses how hybrid spaces may raise new issues of access and digital literacy. The final section of the book concludes with an eye to future technological developments by focusing on trends from the 2014 Mobile World Congress, while also touching on augmented reality technologies like Google Glass and the predicted growth of the "Internet of Things." Most of this book has analyzed the contemporary landscape of location-based services. This concluding chapter links the contemporary moment to a possible future.

Location-based services and the global South

By August, 2013, smartphone penetration had passed 50 percent in 15 countries (Google, 2014). Those countries include the United States and Canada in North America; most of the Western European countries in Europe; Israel, the United Arab Emirates, and Saudi Arabia in the Middle East; Singapore, Hong Kong (which Google's Mobile Project counts as separate from China), and South Korea in Asia; and Australia. Note the absence of African and South American countries on the list. According to the Google Our Mobile Planet project, some global South countries do have widespread smartphone adoption. South African smartphone penetration stands at 39.8 percent of the population, China at 46.9 percent, and Brazil at 26.3 percent (Google, 2014); however, the global South still features lower smartphone adoption than the global North, and analysts expect adoption to increase over the coming years (Gillet, 2013).

While smartphones already seem almost ubiquitous in some parts of the world, the technology is still in the relatively early adopter phase. The "mobile computing revolution" – often dated to the 2007 release of the iPhone (Rowinski, 2014) – is less than a decade old, and worldwide smartphone penetration has already reached 22 percent. Compare that number to the personal computer, which only has a 20 percent penetration rate worldwide despite a longer history (Heggestuen, 2013). Many developing countries, including South Africa and Brazil, already have more smartphones than personal computers, and some background on the traditional mobile phone and what is called "leapfrog technology" can help explain why.

The mobile phone has been the most rapidly adopted technology in history and has been much more widely adopted in the global South than the personal Internet (Castells, Fernandez-Ardevo, Qiu, Jack, and Sey, 2007). For example, a 2011 India census found that 53.2 percent of people owned mobile phones while only 3.2 percent had a home Internet connection (BBC, 2012a). Introducing the mobile phone to local communities does not automatically impact a culture or lead to economic development, despite the deterministic views of some global development agencies (Donner, 2008). However, the mobile phone has helped open up new opportunities in the global South and has helped partially bridge the technological gap between developing and developed nations (Ling and Donner, 2008).

A major reason people in the global South have adopted mobile phones at higher rates than other communication media is because the mobile phone is an example of a "leapfrog" technology (James, 2009).[1] Leapfrogging refers to developing nations "bypassing stages in capacity building or investment through which countries were previously required to pass during the process of economic development" (Steinmueller, 2001: 194). In other words, leapfrogging technologies enable countries to skip a stage in technological development. Mobile phones are one of the most famous examples of leapfrogging (Economist, 2008). Many countries in the global South had little fixed-line phone infrastructure, so they were able to partially skip the fixed-line stage of development and move directly to mobile telephony. The International Telecommunication Union's (ITU)

2013 global technology report found that developing countries only had 11.1 fixed-line subscriptions per 100 residents, as compared to 89.3 mobile phone subscriptions per 100 residents (ITU, 2014). Consequently, while a gap remains in mobile phone adoption between developed and some developing countries, that gap is smaller than it was with fixed-line telephony.

The same situation is now occurring to a lesser degree with the mobile Internet. For many people in the global South, the first time they access the Internet is through their mobile phone, and some commentators have argued that the smartphones and the mobile Internet may "bridge the digital divide" and make access more evenly distributed throughout the world (Ericsson, 2013; Hall, 2013). The world is still a long way from equal access in the developing and developed world, but the rapid increase in smartphone adoption in developing countries such as Brazil, Argentina, and South Africa does suggest that smartphones should at least help people close gaps in global Internet access. The ITU report mentioned earlier found that developing countries have 19.8 mobile broadband subscriptions per 100 people, which is significantly less than in the developed world. However, the number of mobile broadband subscriptions was more than three times as high as the number of fixed-line broadband subscriptions.

One reason smartphone adoption is expected to increase quickly in the developing world is that manufacturers have begun to target less affluent users. A major trend at the 2014 Mobile World Congress – the largest trade show for the mobile industry – was a focus on lower-end smartphones (P.L., 2014). Nokia announced a smartphone that will sell for less than $120, and Mozilla announced a smartphone that will cost only $25, as compared to the typical iPhone or new Samsung phone that sells for more than $600 without a data contract. Lower-end smartphones have been available for years now, but the Mobile World Congress suggests that manufacturers will increasingly focus on affordability as a way to expand into developing markets. As Timo Toikkanen, a vice president at Nokia, argued,

"The fastest growth really is in the affordable smartphone space" (Grundberg, Gryta, and Connors, 2014: para. 7).

Though the development of $25 smartphones will provide access to new groups of users, especially in the developing world, even a $25 smartphone is not a realistic purchase for many groups, despite claims that smartphones will help bridge the digital divide (Ericsson, 2013). A report by the GSMA mWomen project points out that many people in the developing world barely have enough money to provide shelter and food for their families (mWomen, 2012). Many of these people subsist on less than $2 a day, so even a $25 low-end smartphone would cost more than a month's wages, and that does not even include the cost of data fees. In addition, many people in the developing world do not have electricity to charge smartphones even if they could afford them. So while smartphone adoption will bring the mobile Internet to groups of people in the developing world, it is important to recognize that smartphones will likely not come close to actually bridging the digital divide.

While recognizing that smartphones are not a panacea for development, it is fair to note that for many people in the global South who access the Internet primarily through mobile devices, the Internet *is* mobile. They have little experience with personal computers or computer labs. Consequently, many people in the global South who do adopt smartphones will never go through the "placeless" Internet phase discussed in chapter 1, and the Internet they know will likely be closely tied to the types of location-based services discussed in this book. After all, for many people in the global North their associations with the Internet involve a "place" and "time" online. When people went online on their PCs, that time was often seen as separate from the other parts of their lives. If many people in the global South first experience the Internet on smartphones, they will never have that conceptual separation. The Internet will instead begin as something woven into their everyday lives.

People in the global South who are able to adopt smartphones in the future will also likely use location-based services in different ways from many people in the global North. One of the mistakes of deterministic views of technology is the assumption that technologies will have the same impact wherever they are adopted. Instead, different groups shape the meaning and uses of emerging media (Pinch and Bijker, 1987). Mobile phone research in the developing world has shown how Rwandans rely on a modified form of text messaging to bypass economic constraints (Donner, 2007), how Brazilians living in favelas established a culture of sharing surrounding the mobile phone (de Souza e Silva, Sutko, Salis, and C. de Souza e Silva, 2011), and how mobile banking has contributed to a shift in the way that people exchange money in Kenya (Morawczynski, 2009). And those are just a few examples of the huge body of research examining mobile phone adoption in the global South (cf. Donner, 2008).

The near future will see a significant increase in research on how people in the global South adopt smartphones and location-based services, and some locative media research in the global South has already been published, including studies of location-based social networks in China (Hjorth, Wilken, and Gu, 2012), location-based games in Brazil (de Souza e Silva, 2008), and Foursquare use in Indonesia (Glas, 2013). Future research will reveal ways in which people in the global South find unique uses of location-based services, and there will likely be new mobile applications designed specifically for users in different parts of the world. After all, the mobile applications discussed in this book were designed specifically for urban users in industrialized countries (Dourish, Anderson, and Nafus, 2007): LBSNs mainly benefit people with active social lives who have the means to explore new places; Yelp targets users with disposable income to spend at nearby sites of consumption; Google Maps is most useful to people who have the ability to make their own mobility choices to navigate physical space. Most of these mobile applications "focus their attention on young, affluent city residents, with both disposable income and discretionary mobility" (Dourish, Anderson, and Nafus, 2007: 2).

The global South has many people who fit that description. Lagos and Rio de Janeiro both have their urban elite. However, many people will adopt smartphones to accomplish different goals from many users in the developed world. As an article in *The Economist* points out, mobile phone manufacturers and developers recognize that the next wave in smartphone adoption will come in the global South (P.L., 2014). It would be a mistake to assume that the future will see identical uses and identical location-based services as diverse groups adopt smartphones as locative media and begin interacting with and contributing to their hybrid spaces.

The future of splintered space

Unequal access to new communication media, often called the digital divide, has been a central focus of Internet studies. The digital divide refers to divides in access and digital literacy among different countries, as well as divides in access and skills among different groups in the same country. A related concept from mobilities research is the concept of "differential mobility." Differential mobility refers to how access to transportation technologies is differentially distributed amongst groups of people (Wood and Graham, 2005). For example, people of lower socioeconomic classes may be forced into underfunded public transportation because they cannot afford cars. Even if people do own cars, they may not be able to access private highways that charge fees for use. Both the digital divide and differential mobility focus on issues of inequality.

As argued throughout this book, smartphones and location-based services combine the Internet with physical mobility. Consequently, Adriana de Souza e Silva and I (2010b) combined differential mobility with the digital divide to develop the concept of differential space, a concept I later expanded upon and called "splintered space" (Frith, 2012b). Splintered space takes the importance of hybrid spaces as its starting point, and I argued that "what is often lost in discourses about these new understandings of space are questions of who gets to experience this convergence of the digital and the physical" (p. 131). As hybrid spaces become more prominent and more people add to the digital layer of spatial information, researchers and designers need to consider how this will affect people who either do not have the technologies or the skills to take advantage of smartphones and location-based services.

Physical spaces have always been differentially experienced. As a white, male, university professor, I am able to go to places that might be off limits or at least uncomfortable to someone of a different racial, gender, or professional background. The comfortable experience of physical space also requires certain literacy levels: it is much easier to navigate physical space if one can read street signs, store fronts, and other textual markers. Hybrid spaces add a new type of digital literacy to navigating physical space. In conceptual terms, geotagged information exists in servers but is also "attached" to the physical space. That information can include friends' locations, reviews, pictures, traffic updates, directions, or mobile narratives. However, the information is only accessible to people who know it is there and have the right mobile applications and digital literacies to access it.

Imagine two people standing next to each other on the same street corner. One woman has a smartphone and pulls up a location-based service that lets her access nearby geotagged information. The woman stands on the street corner and taps into the information of the hybrid space and reads her surroundings differently. She might read about a nearby restaurant, access a nearby special coupon, map historical places of interest, or find information about a traffic accident a few blocks away. Her space is augmented by the digital information she accesses through her smartphone. Now imagine a man standing next to her. He might own a smartphone but have no idea location-based services exist or how they work. He does not access any of that information about his surrounding space. For the man, the space remains unchanged by the informational layer of the hybrid space. The two people might be standing on the same street corner, but only one of them experiences the physical space in its hybrid form.

These hybrid spaces are not determined by technology (de Souza e Silva, 2006). They are the result of social interactions and social production, not just technological adoption. However, "without access to the right technologies, there is no access to the hybrid space. The space remains unchanged for the millions of people for whom the additional digital information embedded in the physical space may as well not exist" (Frith, 2012b: 133). As the example above suggested, the types of unequal access addressed here are not a simple matter of whether someone owns a smartphone or not. Smartphone ownership is increasing rapidly and will likely do so all over the world, even though access will never come close to reaching a point of utopian equality. More than just demographic issues of access, the near future of splintered space also raises concerns about the types of digital literacy necessary to understand the potential of location-based services to augment experiences of place.

The danger is that new issues of access and literacy are being introduced to public spaces, and as locative media becomes more important to navigating contemporary public spaces, those issues could have serious consequences. Applications have already created coupons that are only available to people with location-based services. Uber is a car service people can use instead of taxis, but only people with the Uber mobile application and a smartphone can order the cars. Universities have created location-based walking tours that guide people through campus, but only people with smartphones can easily access those guides. Cities have created location-based services that direct users to the nearest public transportation and show them how far away a bus is from their physical location, but once again, only people who have the right applications and an adequate level of digital literacy can find that information. And finally, the examples of location-based composition discussed in chapter 6 let new voices contribute to the "durable" layer of information about a place, but that layer only exists for people who know it is there and know how to access it. In the immediate future, society faces the risk of creating "a two-tiered system of city travel: one group will move through malleable, personalised, digitally infused streets, and the other group will move through streets that remain as impersonal as ever" (Frith, 2012b: 141).

The concept of splintered space focuses on more than just whether or not people can access spatial information; it also focuses on concerns about how hybrid spaces may contribute to new forms of personalization. This concern was discussed in chapter 5 in the examination of Alice Crawford's (2007) fears about homogeneity and mobile social networks. Her fears about homogenization can be extended to analyze the spatial customization that individuals face in the near future. As shown throughout this book, location-based services give people control over the types of information they access about their surroundings. People can use their smartphones to filter that information to match their previous searches or their predetermined preferences. In some cases, such as Foursquare's Explore recommendation engine, algorithms do the matching and personalization. What, in effect, could happen is a splintering of how people experience space; two people who use the same application in the same location may each access a totally different set of spatial information.

When someone searches on Google, their results are often personalized based on their past browsing history. They may not even know they do not see the same results as someone else. Facebook also uses algorithms to customize people's News Feed, highlighting stories they may find interesting and not including stories that do not meet certain criteria. And people also do these types of online filtering themselves: they can choose what to follow on Reddit or choose to only go to websites that confirm their world views. This personalization is what Eli Pariser (2011) calls the "filter bubble," and he fears that these types of online customization may limit people's perspectives. As sociologist Sivaid Vaidhyanathan (2011) warned in his description of Google's search algorithm:

if search results are more customized, you are less likely to stumble on the unexpected, the unknown, the unfamiliar, and the uncomfortable. Your Web search experience will reinforce whatever affiliations, interests, opinions, and biases you already possess. (p. 183)

Returning to the earlier example of two people standing on the same street corner can illustrate how this concern can be extended to locative media. This time imagine both individuals use smartphones and they both have access to a variety of location-based services. They both pull up a spatial search application and search for nearby locations. Even though they are standing in the same spot and using the same location-based service, they receive different results customized through a search algorithm that matches them to places that best match their previous habits. One person receives a special alert pointing her to a sale at the nearby bookstore because her browsing history includes visits to Amazon.com. The other person receives an alert about an upcoming show at a music venue a block away because he liked a few local bands on Facebook. The first user might have no idea the music venue that is one street over even exists, and the second person might never be made aware of the nearby bookstore. They stand in the same location using the same application, but their experience of place is customized for them. They use locative media to bring their "filter bubbles" out into physical space.

These two related concerns – digital inequality and customization – are both important issues facing the future of locative media. This book has mostly focused on positive uses of location-based services, and people will continue to find interesting ways to use location to explore new forms of social networking, mobile composition, and navigation. However, there is a possible future in which space splinters in new ways, especially if location-based services become an even more important part of how people experience place. In the near future, people might turn to their smartphones as the primary tool for finding new places and navigating routes. It matters if algorithms customize their experiences and provide certain people with information not available to others. Society also faces a future in which mobile applications like Uber may begin to replace existing infrastructure, so it matters if groups of people are left out of these developments because they either do not have smartphones or do not have certain digital literacies. Emerging media often introduce new questions of inequality and access; smartphones as locative media are no different.

Possible futures of locative media

Making bold predictions about the future of technology is risky. Intelligent people predicted the personal computer would never be popular, satellites would never be used for communication, and the Internet would be a passing fad (Fogarty, 2012). However, predicting the near future of smartphones and location-based services is made easier by examining the trends at the annual Mobile World Congress mentioned earlier in this chapter. The Mobile World Congress is held in February each year in Barcelona, Spain, and is the largest exhibition of the mobile industry, bringing together executives, software developers, carriers, and consumers. This final section begins by discussing a few of the trends of the conference before concluding with a more speculative discussion of the future of smartphones and location-based services.

As discussed earlier, one of the major trends at the Mobile World Congress was a focus on lower-end, affordable smartphones. The event also featured newer, more high-end mobile technologies, including augmented reality (AR) mobile applications. AR refers to the overlay of digital information on physical space (Manovich, 2006), and AR applications are a still small subset of location-based services. Applications like Layar and Google Ingress allow people to point their phones at a location, see an image of the location on their mobile screen, and then place digital information over the image. AR has yet to be widely adopted, but the 2013 beta release of Google Glass suggests a possible next step in the development of AR and locative media. Google Glass is a set of glasses people wear that then overlays digital information on their surrounding space, and it requires location awareness to locate the user and augment their surroundings. AR was not addressed in this book because Google Glass is still in the beta testing stage, and there are concerns that it may never be widely adopted (Baldwin, 2012). However, the AR model used by Google Glass does suggest one possible future for locative media.

Another trend in mobile technologies found at the Mobile World Congress is an increasing push towards the realization of the "Internet of Things." The Internet of Things is a framework in which billions of objects are given unique identifiers and Internet capability. These objects will form a network and in some cases be able to connect with one another. There are already many examples of the growing Internet of Things, and to spot examples look for any object marketed with the adjective "smart" before its name. "Smart" thermostats, "smart" cars, and "smart" appliances already exist. The Mobile World Congress also highlighted an increasing focus on "smart" wearable technologies, including wrist bands to monitor people's heart rate and fitness level (P.L., 2014). A *Business Insider* report estimated that 1.9 billion devices – ranging from thermostats to parking meters – are already connected to the Internet (Adler, 2013), and research firm Gartner forecasts that 26 billion devices will be connected by 2020 (Gartner, 2013).

While it is still not clear what people are supposed to do with smart refrigerators, it is clear that there will be an increase in networked objects. These objects will form the networks imagined in the Internet of Things, and as argued by Simon Segars, CEO of British technology company ARM, smartphones will likely be a "'hub' from which other connected gadgets will be controlled" (P.L., 2014: para. 4). This model of an Internet of networked objects connecting to and through smartphones will require near constant location awareness. The smartphone will be locatable in order to interact with nearby "smart" objects (Greenfield,

2006), though the location awareness will likely rely on networks of sensors just as much as it does on GPS and Wi-Fi triangulation. As a hub in these networks of "smart" objects, the locative aspect of smartphones may become increasingly invisible. Rather than opening up location-based services and waiting for location information, the smartphone may just be located at all times as it moves through networks of sensors built into objects in the everyday world.[2]

That type of seamlessness suggests a future in which a book like this would not even be necessary, a future in which users will not consider location-based services as something separate worth discussing. Instead, location awareness will be incorporated into most networked interactions, operating invisibly in the background. Possibly the most coherent vision of how this future might look can be found in the 2013 Spike Jonze film *Her*, which imagined a near future in which a man falls in love with a sentient mobile operating system. The main character – Theodore Twombly – interacts seamlessly with his mobile device. He transitions between calls, emails, and information about his surroundings, and the digital data he accesses is not at all separate from his interactions with the physical world. He does not wait for GPS signals or Wi-Fi triangulation; instead, the mobile device, his operating system in this case, knows when to give him information and knows what types of information will interest him, a model now being explored by the Google Now service available on Android phones that passively delivers information to users based on what the algorithm predicts the user will want (e.g., how long it will take to drive home from the user's location). *Her* combines the Internet of Things with an augmented reality future that imagines the types of interactions with the physical world that are present in Google Glass's promotional videos. The movie also turns away from the application model covered in this book. Instead, all of Twombly's interactions with augmented data are seamlessly connected rather than contained in the silos of individual applications. Ultimately, the mobile OS as locative media is never remarked upon in the film because the location awareness is taken for granted.

Society is still a long way from the seamless future of *Her*. People still rely on the mobile application ecosystem detailed in this book, with different applications serving different purposes. That will not change in the immediate future, and users will still turn to different applications to provide different types of information about their surroundings. But there will likely be a future in which smartphones are even more closely interwoven with everyday interactions and location information is passively present in most interactions with mobile devices. For now, however, people will continue to use their individual location-based services, and physical spaces will continue to be filled with even denser layers of digital spatial information. And, as this book has argued, possibly the most significant social impact of the growth of smartphones as locative media involves the new ways in which the merging of the digital and physical have impacted people's experience of place.

Whatever the future holds, the next five years will be an exciting time for people interested in smartphones and location-based services. I started studying locative media five years ago, and much has changed during that time. There are now over 1 million mobile applications, and smartphone ownership has increased rapidly. Applications that were cutting edge then are now enfolded into the daily routines of everyday users. But however much location-based services have changed, much remains the same. People still use their smartphones to access mobile maps, contribute socially produced spatial information, and find their friends, just as they did in 2008. The applications they use to accomplish these goals look different and function differently, but the core behaviors remain fairly similar. The next five years will see an explosion of new applications and a possible move towards the Internet of Things and Augmented Reality technologies. Smartphone ownership will grow in the global South and new forms of location-based services will be created to meet the needs of different groups. The mobile application ecosystem will almost certainly be different from this contemporary moment; however, it will also share similarities with the applications discussed in this book, even as people find new ways to interact with and contribute to the future of hybrid spaces.

Notes

CHAPTER I FROM ATOMS TO BITS AND BACK AGAIN

1 The tendency to oppose the virtual to the physical also often ignored the huge amount of physical infrastructure on which digital networks rely. See Andrew Blum's (2013) *Tubes: A Journey to the Center of the Internet* for an excellent account of that infrastructure.

2 Hybrid space is not the only concept that views digital location-based information as intertwined with physical space. Lev Manovich's (2006) concept of augmented reality and Rob Kitchin and Martin Dodge's (2011) concept of code/space also refuse the urge to separate the two. While I focus on hybrid space throughout the book, both these works provide similar analyses of the ways in which digital information is increasingly shaping how people experience the physical world.

CHAPTER 2 MOBILITIES AND THE SPATIAL TURN

1 Michel de Certeau's work on space and place reverses the two terms. As Cresswell (2004) describes, "Confusingly for geographers, de Certeau uses space and place in a way that stands the normal distinction on its head" (p. 38).

2 Paul Dourish (2006) later updated his argument to recognize how space is also socially produced by various technologies of mapping.

3 For a longer explanation of the analysis detailed in this section, please see chapters 1 and 2 of de Souza e Silva and my (2012) book *Mobile Interfaces in Public Spaces*.

CHAPTER 3 THE INFRASTRUCTURE OF LOCATIVE MEDIA

1 Google uses Streetview to record the addresses of Wi-Fi routers to improve Google Location Services. The practice became controversial when it was revealed that Google was also intercepting unencrypted data from open Wi-Fi routers, and Google was fined by privacy commissions in Italy and Germany for accessing the unencrypted data (Miller and O'Brien, 2013).

2 The iPhone was not Apple's first phone. In 2005, Apple released the ROKR phone in a joint venture with Motorola, but the ROKR was widely regarded as a disappointment (Goggin, 2009). The phone did not feature a touch screen and mainly focused on integrating with the Apple music store.

3 For an in-depth history of the Simon smartphone, see Sager (2012).

4 While Android dominates market share, Apple makes far more money from the iPhone than Google does from Android (Bradley, 2013).

5 Apple works with a company named Foxconn to assemble iPhones and iPads. Foxconn has been criticized for what are widely perceived as exploitative labor practices in China (Guglielmo, 2013).

6 Android was not the first open-source smartphone operating system. In 2008, Nokia purchased the Symbian operating system and created the Symbian Foundation. The Foundation then made Symbian open source and royalty free (Goggin, 2012).

7 Google was one of the founding members of the Open Handset Alliance (OHA), which is a consortium formed in 2007 to develop open-source approaches for mobile devices. Android is the most famous result of the OHA.

CHAPTER 4 WAYFINDING THROUGH MOBILE INTERFACES

1 The 2010 border dispute between Nicaragua and Costa Rica is another example of the importance of lines on maps. Google Maps had wrongly labeled the Calero Island in Costa Rica as part of Nicaragua. Nicaragua then sent 50 troops to the island and claimed it was part of Nicaragua, despite Costa Rican protests. The dispute was later settled, avoiding what some called the "first Google Maps war" (F. Jacobs, 2012).

2 A post from Charlie Hale (2010), Geo Policy Analyst at Google,

explained how complicated it can be for Google Maps to make choices about disputed territories. The post is worth reading in its entirety for anyone interested in how mapmakers incorporate political controversies in their maps.

3   Jorge Luis Borges's short story "On the exactitude of science" is an interesting thought experiment that shows why a map can never truly capture the territory it represents. The story is about the perfect map, one that is literally as large as the territory it represents so that it can capture everything. The map cannot fully represent the territory without literally becoming the territory.

4   Even the world map people see all the time is one of many possible representations. The typical world map is called the Mercator Projection, which has shaped the way people understand the world, but like with any map, it represents a set of choices. The Mercator Projection preserves the shape of land masses, which makes it a useful representation of the world for navigation purposes (Dourish, 2006). However, the Mercator Projection distorts the size of land masses by making land in the northern hemisphere appear larger than land in the southern hemisphere. If you look at a typical world map, say Google Maps, it appears as if Greenland is bigger than Africa. Europe appears to be slightly larger than South America. However, the Mercator Projection is a choice, not a direct representation of the world. In reality, Africa is far larger than Greenland, and South America dwarfs the land mass of Europe. The Peters Map is an alternative to the Mercator Projection and attempts to maintain the relative size of land masses, meaning that many land masses of the southern hemisphere appear much larger than on the Mercator Projection (Wood, 1992).

5   Another example of the potential consequences of letting only a few huge companies control our maps is the Microsoft "dynamic walking" patent. Microsoft filed for a patent for an algorithm that will give people "safe" walking routes, telling them to avoid streets with crime rates over a certain threshold. Some critics immediately labeled the technology as the "avoid the ghetto" feature and called the service racist (Keyes, 2012). Whether the feature is racist or not, it is a reminder that people need multiple mapping applications so that those kinds of decisions are not made for them.

CHAPTER 5   LOCATION AND SOCIAL NETWORKS

1   Here is the link to the commercial: <http://www.youtube.com/ watch?v=BziaRelGgTg>.

2   Interestingly, location sharing can also be used to *avoid* coordination. The application Cloak bills itself as an "anti-social network" that draws from Foursquare and Facebook to help people avoid running into friends.

3   For a detailed analysis of different definitions of public space, see J. Weintraub (1997).

4   Grindr and Tinder are two of many location-based dating applications. Other examples include MeetMoi, Skout, and Zoost. Large online dating websites, including OkCupid and PlentyofFish, also have mobile applications that use location information.

5   Blog: <http://4sqlovestory.com/>.

CHAPTER 7   MARKET FORCES AND THE SHAPING OF LOCATION-BASED SERVICES

1   Much of this section is derived from Austin Carr's (2013b) excellent, in-depth profile of Foursquare co-founder Dennis Crowley.

2   The location tagging on Twitter, as opposed to Vine, mostly relies on actual geotagging rather than Foursquare's user-generated location database. So when someone adds location to their tweet, they add the longitude and latitude, though they can also share more general locations like their city or neighborhood.

CHAPTER 8   THE NEGOTIATION OF LOCATIONAL PRIVACY

1   This divide also fits with a study performed by de Souza e Silva and me (2010a) on four months of media discourse about location-based services.

2   Verizon has since removed this language from its description of the program. However, the old language can be accessed here: <http://business.verizonwireless.com/content/b2b/en/precision/precision-market-insights.html>.

3   Warden and Allan released an open-source program called iPhone Tracker that displayed the data from the location file on a map to show users just how revealing a persistent log of their location can be. iPhone Tracker can be downloaded here: <http://petewarden.github.io/iPhoneTracker/>.

4   The blog post stressed that Foursquare users have control over the data they share, while also acknowledging that there can be downsides

to location sharing. The post also pointed out that someone probably does not need to check Foursquare to see if someone is home or not. They can simply log in to Twitter and search for phrases like "heading to …"

CONCLUSION: THE FUTURE OF LOCATIVE MEDIA

1   Another major reason mobile telephony has taken off in the developing world is the growth of prepaid plans (Castells, Fernandez-Ardevo, Qiu, Jack, and Sey, 2007). Many people do not have the stable income to pay the monthly subscription fees popular in the global North. Prepaid plans allow people to pay up-front for a certain number of voice minutes and text messages. Prepaid smartphone plans that include data caps are now becoming more popular in the global South and the global North, opening up opportunities for people without stable income to use the mobile Internet (Ericsson, 2012).

2   The model for this type of seamless location awareness traces back to the 1990s and the "calm computing" movement in which computing disappears into the background (Weiser, Gold, and Brown, 1999). For example, computer scientists in the mid-1990s were already exploring "smart houses" in which sensors would detect people's location and alter settings such as temperature and lighting to match their predetermined settings. A more dystopian example of this seamless future is the data service Turnstyle that set up sensors throughout businesses in Toronto. The sensors collected data about the phones that were close enough to the sensors, and the data was then sold to businesses. The smartphone users had no idea their data was being collected because the process worked seamlessly, and the sensors that are part of the Internet of Things will collect more data that can be used by private companies to enhance the marketing schemes discussed in chapter 8 (K. Crawford, 2014).

References

About Foursquare. (2014). Retrieved from <https://foursquare.com/about/>.

ACLU. (2011). ACLU public records analysis. *American Civil Liberties Union*. Retrieved from <https://www.aclu.org/files/assets/cell_phone_tracking_documents_-_final.pdf>.

ACLU. (2012). Cell phone location tracking public records request. *American Civil Liberties Union*. Retrieved from <https://www.aclu.org/protecting-civil-liberties-digital-age/cell-phone-location-tracking-public-records-request>.

Adler, E. (2013). Here's why "the Internet of Things" will be huge, and drive tremendous value for people and businesses. *Business Insider*. Retrieved from <http://www.businessinsider.com/growth-in-the-internet-of-things-2013-10>.

Agar, J. (2005). *Constant Touch: A Global History of the Mobile Phone*. Cambridge, MA: Totem Publishers.

Agnew, J. (2011). Space and place. In J. Agnew and D. Livingstone (eds), *Handbook of Geographical Knowledge*. London: Sage, pp. 316–30.

Agnew, J., and Duncan, J. (1989). *The Power of Place: Bringing Together Geographical and Sociological Imaginations*. London: Unwin Hyman.

Akrich, M. (1992). The de-scription of technical objects. In W. E. Bijker and J. Law (eds), *Shaping Technology/Building Society: Studies in Sociotechnical Change*. Cambridge, MA: MIT Press, pp. 205–24.

Amadeo, R. (2013). Google's iron grip on Android: Controlling open source by any means necessary. *Ars Technica*. Retrieved from <http://arstechnica.com/gadgets/2013/10/googles-iron-grip-on-android-controlling-open-source-by-any-means-necessary/>.

Anderson, C., and Wolff, M. (2010). The web is dead. Long live the Internet. *Wired*. Retrieved from <http://www.wired.com/magazine/2010/08/ff_webrip/>.

Anderson, J. (2014). The biggest winner at the Winter Olympics is Tinder. *USA Today*. Retrieved from <http://ftw.usatoday.com/2014/02/the-biggest-winner-at-the-winter-olympics-is-tinder/>.

Angwin, J., and Valentino-Devries, J. (2011). Apple, Google collect user data. *The Wall Street Journal*. Retrieved from <http://online.wsj.com/news/articles/SB10001424052748703983704576277101723453610>.

Ante, S. E. (2010). Foursquare locates new funds to expand. *The Wall Street Journal*. Retrieved from <http://online.wsj.com/news/articles/SB10001424052748704846004575333222375027784>.

Ante, S. E. (2012). Investors cool on Foursquare. *The Wall Street Journal*. Retrieved from <http://online.wsj.com/news/articles/SB10001424127887324712504578131384140607240>.

Apple. (2014). App review. *Apple.com*. Retrieved from <https://developer.apple.com/appstore/guidelines.html>.

Arthur, C. (2011). iPhone keeps record of everywhere you go. *The Guardian*. Retrieved from <http://www.theguardian.com/technology/2011/apr/20/iphone-tracking-prompts-privacy-fears>.

Augé, M. (1995). *Non-Places: An Introduction to Supermodernity*. London: Verso.

Bakdash, J. Z., Linkenauger, S. A., and Proffitt, D. (2008). Comparing decision-making and control for learning a virtual environment: Backseat drivers learn where they are going. *Proceedings of the Human Factors and Ergonomics Society Annual Meeting* 52/27: 2117–21.

Baldwin, R. (2012). Google Glasses face serious hurdles, augmented-reality experts say. *Gadget Lab | Wired*. Retrieved from <http://www.wired.com/gadgetlab/2012/04/augmented-reality-experts-say-google-glasses-face-serious-hurdles/>.

Barouch, J. (2013). Foursquare's API is a pillar of the mobile app ecosystem. *TechCrunch*. Retrieved from <http://techcrunch.com/2013/03/29/the-internet-needs-foursquare-to-succeed/>.

Baym, N. (2010). *Personal Connections in the Digital Age*. Cambridge: Polity.

BBC. (2012a). No toilet in half of Indian homes. *BBC News*. Retrieved from <http://www.bbc.co.uk/news/world-asia-india-17362837>.

BBC. (2012b). Telefonica plans "big data" arm. *BBC*. Retrieved from <http://www.bbc.co.uk/news/technology-19882647>.

Beadon, L. (2012). Google Maps exodus continues as Wikipedia mobile applications switch to OpenStreetMap. *Techdirt*. Retrieved from <http://www.techdirt.com/articles/20120405/17321218398/google-maps-exodus-continues-as-wikipedia-mobile-applications-switch-to-openstreetmap.shtml>.

Bengtsson, L., Lu, X., Thorson, A., Garfield, R., and Schreeb, J. V. (2011). Improved response to disasters and outbreaks by tracking population movements with mobile phone network data: A post-earthquake geospatial study in Haiti. *PLOS Medicine* 8/8. Retrieved from <http://www.ncbi.nlm.nih.gov/pubmed/21918643>.

Bensinger, G., and Calia, M. (2013). Amazon reports another loss despite

24% revenue growth. *The Wall Street Journal*. Retrieved from <http://
online.wsj.com/news/articles/SB1000142405270230479940457915584
3622506978>.

Benzow, G. (2011). Cyber sweep costs Dresden police chief his job. *DW.DE*.
Retrieved from <http://www.dw.de/cyber-sweep-costs-dresden-police-
chief-his-job/a-15192763-1>.

Bertel, T. F. (2013a). "It's like I trust it so much that I don't really check
where it is I'm going before I leave": Informational uses of smartphones
among Danish youth. *Mobile Media and Communication* 1/3: 299–313.

Bertel, T. F. (2013b). *Mobile Communication in the Age of Smartphones:
Processes of Domestication and Re-domestication* (Dissertation). IT
University of Copenhagen, Copenhagen, Denmark.

Best, J. (2007). Nokia tops in 2006 smartphone sales. *Business Week*.
Retrieved from <http://www.businessweek.com/stories/2007-02-27/
nokia-tops-in-2006-smartphone-salesbusinessweek-business-news-sto
ck-market-and-financial-advice>.

Bilton, R. (2013). The new, more amazing Foursquare is about the money
– not the mayorships. *VentureBeat*. Retrieved from <http://venturebeat.
com/2013/03/20/new-foursquare/>.

Blaze, M. (2012). House committee on the judiciary subcommittee
on crime, terrorism, and homeland security hearing on ECPA, part
2: Geolocation privacy and surveillance. *House.gov*. Retrieved from
<http://judiciary.house.gov/hearings/113th/04252013/Blaze%200425
2013.pdf>.

Bloom, H. (1988). *The Closing of the American Mind*. New York: Simon &
Schuster.

Blum, A. (2013). *Tubes: A Journey to the Center of the Internet*. New York:
Ecco.

Blumberg, A. J., and Eckersley, P. (2009). On locational privacy and how
to avoid losing it forever. *Electronic Frontier Foundation*. Retrieved from
<https://www.eff.org/wp/locational-privacy>.

Boesen, J., Rode, J. A., and Mancini, C. (2010). The domestic panopticon:
Location tracking in families. In *Proceedings of the 12th ACM International
Conference on Ubiquitous Computing*. New York: ACM, pp. 65–74.

boyd, d. (2007). Why youth <3 social network sites: The role of networked
publics in teenage social life. In D. Buckingham (ed.), *Youth, Identity,
and Digital Media*. Cambridge, MA: MIT Press, pp. 119–42.

boyd, d. (2008). Facebook's privacy trainwreck. *Convergence: The
International Journal of Research into New Media Technologies* 14/1:
13–20.

boyd, d. (2011). Debating privacy in a networked world for the WSJ. *danah
boyd | Apophenia*. Retrieved from <http://www.zephoria.org/thoughts/

archives/2011/11/20/debating-privacy-in-a-networked-world-for-the-wsj. html>.

boyd, d., and Ellison, N. (2008). Social network sites: Definition, history, and scholarship. *Journal of Computer-Mediated Communication* 13/1: 210–30.

boyd, d., and Hargittai, E. (2010). Facebook privacy settings: Who cares? *First Monday* 15/8. Retrieved from <http://firstmonday.org/article/ view/3086/2589>.

Bradley, T. (2013). Android dominates market share, but Apple makes all the money. *Forbes*. Retrieved from <http://www.forbes.com/sites/tony bradley/2013/11/15/android-dominates-market-share-but-apple-makes-all-the-money/>.

Brehm, D. (2012). Cellphone data helps pinpoint source of traffic tie-ups. *MIT News Office*. Retrieved from <http://newsoffice.mit.edu/2012/cell phone-data-helps-pinpoint-source-of-traffic-tie-ups-1220>.

Brownlee, J. (2012). This creepy app isn't just stalking women without their knowledge. *Cult of Mac*. Retrieved from <http://www.cultofmac. com/157641/this-creepy-app-isnt-just-stalking-women-without-their-kn owledge-its-a-wake-up-call-about-facebook-privacy/>.

Buchanon, M. (2010). The dirty secret of today's 4G: It's not 4G. *Gizmodo*. Retrieved from <http://gizmodo.com/5680755/the-dirty-secret-of-todays-4g-its-not-4g>.

Bull, M. (2000). *Sounding Out the City: Personal Stereos and the Management of Everyday Life*. Oxford: Berg.

Bull, M. (2004). Thinking about sound, proximity, and distance in western experience: The case of Odysseus's Walkman. In V. Erlmann (ed.), *Hearing Cultures: Essays on Sound, Listening, and Modernity*. New York: Berg, pp. 173–90.

Bull, M. (2006). Investigating the culture of mobile listening: From Walkman to iPod. In K. O'Hara and B. Brown (eds), *Consuming Music Together: Social and Collaborative Aspects of Music Consumption Technologies*. New York: Springer, pp. 131–49.

Bull, M. (2007). *Sound Moves: iPod Culture and Urban Experience*. New York: Routledge.

Carey, J. (1989). *Communication as Culture*. New York: Routledge.

Carlson, N. (2010). Foursquare doomed? Facebook Places has 7x more users. *Business Insider*. Retrieved from <http://www.businessinsider. com/facebook-places-may-have-30-million-users-but-none-of-them-use-it-very-much-2010-10>.

Carlson, N. (2011). Foursquare raises $50 million at $600 million valuation. *Business Insider*. Retrieved from <http://www.businessinsider. com/foursquare-raises-50-million-at-600-million-valuation-2011-6>.

Carr, A. (2013a). Foursquare's new app brings search to forefront, nixes social feed. *Fast Company*. Retrieved from <http://www.fastcompany.com/3016165/foursquares-new-app-bring-search-to-forefront-nixes-social-feed>.

Carr, A. (2013b). Will Foursquare CEO Dennis Crowley finally get it right? *Fast Company*. Retrieved from <http://www.fastcompany.com/3014821/will-foursquare-ceo-dennis-crowley-finally-get-it-right>.

Casey, E. (1996). How to get from space to place in a fairly short stretch of time. In S. Feld and K. Baso (eds), *Sense of Place*. Santa Fe, NM: School of American Research.

Cashmore, P. (2009). Next year's Twitter? It's Foursquare. Retrieved from <http://edition.cnn.com/2009/TECH/11/19/cashmore.foursquare/>.

Cashmore, P. (2010). Facebook steals Foursquare's location crown. *CNN*. Retrieved from <http://www.cnn.com/2010/TECH/social.media/08/19/cashmore.facebook.places/index.html>.

Castells, M. (2000). *The Rise of the Network Society*. Oxford: Blackwell.

Castells, M., Fernandez-Ardevo, M., Qiu, M., Jack, L., and Sey, A. (2007). *Mobile Communication and Society: A Global Perspective*. Cambridge, MA: MIT Press.

Chen, B. (2008). Android welcomes App Store's rejects with arms wide open. *Wired*. Retrieved from <http://www.wired.com/2008/09/will-google-and/>.

Chen, B. X. (2011). *Always On: How the iPhone Unlocked the Anything-Anytime-Anywhere Future – and Locked Us In*. New York: Da Capo Press.

Consolvo, S., Smith, I. E., Matthews, T., LaMarca, A., Tabert, J., and Powledge, P. (2005). Location disclosure to social relations: Why, when, and what people want to share. In *Proceedings of the SIGCHI Conference on Human Factors in Computing Systems*. New York: ACM, pp. 81–90.

Couldry, N., and McCarthy, A. (eds). (2004). *MediaSpace: Place, Scale and Culture in a Media Age*. New York: Routledge.

Cramer, H., Rost, M., and Holmquist, E. (2011). Performing a check-in: Emerging practices, norms and "conflicts" in location-sharing using Foursquare. In *MobileHCI 2011*.

Crawford, A. (2007). Taking social software to the streets: Mobile cocooning and the (an)erotic city. *Journal of Urban Technology* 15/3: 79–97.

Crawford, K. (2014). When big data marketing becomes stalking. *Scientific American*. Retrieved from <http://www.scientificamerican.com/article/when-big-data-marketing-becomes-stalking/>.

Cresswell, T. (2004). *Place: A Short Introduction*. Malden, MA: Blackwell.

Cresswell, T. (2010). Towards a politics of mobility. *Environment and Planning D: Society and Space* 28/1: 17–31.

Crowley, D. (2007). Me + alex quit google. (dodgeball forever!!!!). *Flickr*. Retrieved from <http://www.flickr.com/photos/dpstyles/460987802/>.

Crowley, D. (2013). Continuing Foursquare's growth. *Foursquare Blog*. Retrieved from <http://blog.foursquare.com/2013/04/11/continuing-foursquares-growth/>.

Crump, C. (2013). Federal appeals court rules the government can track your cell phone without a warrant. *American Civil Liberties Union*. Retrieved from <https://www.aclu.org/blog/technology-and-liberty/federal-appeals-court-rules-government-can-track-your-cell-phone-without>.

Curwen, P. (2002). *The Future of Mobile Communication: Awaiting the Third Generation*. New York: Palgrave.

Daily Mail. (2011). Who's listening to your calls? *The Daily Mail*. Retrieved from <http://www.dailymail.co.uk/news/article-2055543/Whos-listening-Met-police-track-thousands-mobiles-using-covert-surveillance-system.html>.

Danchik, R. J. (1988). An overview of TRANSIT development. *Johns Hopkins APL Technical Digest* 19/1: 18–26.

de Certeau, M. (1988). *The Practice of Everyday Life*. Minneapolis, MN: University of Minnesota Press.

de Gournay, C. (2002). Pretense of intimacy in France. In J. Katz and M. Aakhus (eds), *Perpetual Contact: Mobile Communication, Private Talk, Public Performance*. Cambridge: Cambridge University Press.

de Souza e Silva, A. (2006). From cyber to hybrid: Mobile technologies as interfaces of hybrid spaces. *Space and Culture* 3: 261–78.

de Souza e Silva, A. (2008). Alien Revolt: A case-study of the first location-based mobile game in Brazil. *IEEE Technology and Society Magazine* 27/1: 18–28.

de Souza e Silva, A., and Frith, J. (2010a). Locational privacy in public spaces: Media discourses on the personalization and control of space by location-aware mobile media. *Communication, Culture and Critique* 3/4: 503–25.

de Souza e Silva, A., and Frith, J. (2010b). Locative mobile social networks: Mapping communication and location in urban spaces. *Mobilities* 5/4: 485–505.

de Souza e Silva, A., and Frith, J. (2012). *Mobile Interfaces in Public Spaces: Locational Privacy, Control and Urban Sociability*. New York: Routledge.

de Souza e Silva, A., and Frith, J. (2013). Re-narrating the city through the presentation of location. In J. Farman (ed.), *The Mobile Story: Narrative Practices with Locative Technologies*. New York: Routledge, pp. 34–50.

de Souza e Silva, A., and Sutko, D. (2011). Theorizing locative technologies through philosophies of the virtual. *Communication Theory* 21/1: 23–42.

de Souza e Silva, A., Sutko, D. M., Salis, F. A., and de Souza e Silva, C. (2011). Mobile phone appropriation in the favelas of Rio de Janeiro, Brazil. *New Media & Society* 13/3: 411–26.

Donner, J. (2007). The rules of beeping: Exchanging messages using missed calls on mobile phones in sub-Saharan Africa. *Journal of Computer-Mediated Communication* 13/1: 1–22.

Donner, J. (2008). Research approaches to mobile use in the developing world: A review of the literature. *The Information Society* 24/3: 140–59.

Dourish, P. (2006). Re-space-ing place: "Place" and "Space" ten years on. In *Proceedings of the 2006 20th Anniversary Conference on Computer Supported Cooperative Work*. Banff, Canada: ACM.

Dourish, P., and Bell, G. (2011). *Divining a Digital Future*. Cambridge, MA: MIT Press.

Dourish, P., Anderson, K., and Nafus, D. (2007). Cultural mobilities: Diversity and agency in urban computing. *Lecture Notes in Computer Science* 4663: 100–13.

Du Gay, P., Hall, S., Janes, L., Mackay, H., and Negus, K. (1997). *Doing Cultural Studies: The Story of the Sony Walkman*. London: Sage.

Duggan, M. (2013). *Cell Phone Activities 2013*. PEW Internet and American Life. Retrieved from <http://www.pewinternet.org/~/media/Files/Reports/2013/PIP_Cell%20Phone%20Activities%20May%202013.pdf>.

Duryee, T. (2008). 3G Adoption in the U.S. Exceeds Western Europe: Report. *Washington Post*. Retrieved from <http://articles.washingtonpost.com/2008-09-03/news/36805919_1_3g-penetration-total-subscribers>.

Eagle, N., and Pentland, A. (2004). *Social Serendipity: Proximity Sensing and Cueing*. Cambridge, MA: MIT Media Laboratory. Retrieved from <http://hd.media.mit.edu/tech-reports/old-TR-580.pdf>.

Economist. (2008). The limits of leapfrogging. *The Economist*. Retrieved from <http://www.economist.com/node/10650775>.

Efrati, A., and Rubin, B. F. (2013). Google confirms Waze maps app purchase. *The Wall Street Journal*. Retrieved from <http://online.wsj.com/news/articles/SB10001424127887323949990457853937098068606106>.

Eisenstein, E. (1979). *The Printing Press as an Agent of Change*. Cambridge: Cambridge University Press.

eMarketer. (2013). Real-time location data gets a bigger slice of mobile targeting. *Emarketer*. Retrieved from <http://www.emarketer.com/Article/Real-Time-Location-Data-Gets-Bigger-Slice-of-Mobile-Targeting/1009675>.

Engestrom, Y. (1991). Activity theory and individual and social transformation. In Y. Engestrom, R. Miettenien, and R. L. Punamäki-Gitai (eds),

Perspectives on Activity Theory. New York: Cambridge University Press, pp. 19–39.

Ericsson. (2012). *Profitable Prepaid Smartphones*. Ericsson. Retrieved from <http://www.ericsson.com/res/region_RASO/docs/2012/ericsson_prepaid_paper_june.pdf>.

Ericsson. (2013). *Bridging the Digital Divide*. Ericsson ConsumerLabs. Retrieved from <http://www.ericsson.com/res/docs/2013/consumerlab/bridging-the-digital-divide-sub-saharan-africa.pdf>.

Farman, J. (2010). Mapping the digital empire: Google Earth and the process of postmodern cartography. *New Media & Society* 12/6: 869–88.

Farman, J. (2012). *Mobile Interface Theory*. New York: Routledge.

Farman, J. (2013). *The Mobile Story: Narrative Practices with Locative Technologies*. New York: Routledge.

Fiegerman, S. (2013). Google play passes 50 billion app downloads. *Mashable*. Retrieved from <http://mashable.com/2013/07/18/google-play-50-billion-applications/>.

Fischer, C. S. (1994). *America Calling: A Social History of the Telephone to 1940*. Berkeley and Los Angeles, CA: University of California Press.

Flamm, M. (2013). Foursquare doesn't quite check out. *Crain's New York Business*. Retrieved from <http://www.crainsnewyork.com/article/20130120/TECHNOLOGY/301209972>.

Flanders, J. (2006). Hooked on books. *Guardian*. Retrieved from <http://www.telegraph.co.uk/culture/books/3654668/Hooked-on-books.html>.

Fogarty, K. (2012). Tech predictions gone wrong. *Computerworld*. Retrieved from <http://www.computerworld.com/s/article/9232610/Tech_predictions_gone_wrong>.

Foursquare. (2010). On Foursquare, location and privacy . . . *Foursquare*. Retrieved from <http://foursquare.tumblr.com/post/397625136/on-foursquare-location-privacy>.

Foursquare. (2014). A look into the future of Foursquare, including a new app called Swarm. Retrieved from <http://blog.foursquare.com/post/84422758243/a-look-into-the-future-of-foursquare-including-a-new>.

Frith, J. (2012a). *Constructing Location, One Check-in at a Time: Examining the Practices of Foursquare Users* (Dissertation). North Carolina State University, Raleigh, NC. Retrieved from <http://repository.lib.ncsu.edu/ir/bitstream/1840.16/8064/1/etd.pdf>.

Frith, J. (2012b). Splintered space: Hybrid spaces and differential mobility. *Mobilities* 7/1: 131–49.

Frith, J. (2013). Turning life into a game: Foursquare, gamification, and personal mobility. *Mobile Media and Communication* 1/2: 248–62.

Frith, J. (2014). Communicating through location: The understood meaning of the Foursquare check-in. *Journal of Computer-Mediated Communication*; doi:10.1177/1354856514527191.

Frith, J. (in press). Writing space: Examining the potential of location-based composition. *Computers and Composition*.

Frith, J., and Kalin, J. (in press). Here, I used to be: Mobile media and practices of place-based digital memory. *Space and Culture*.

Gallo, C. (2011). *The Power of Foursquare*. New York: McGraw Hill.

Garde-Hansen, J., Hoskins, A., and Reading, A. (2009). *Save as . . . Digital Memories*. New York: Palgrave Macmillan.

Gartner. (2013). The Internet of Things' installed base will grow to 26 billion units by 2020. *Gartner*. Retrieved from <http://www.gartner.com/newsroom/id/2636073>.

Gartner. (2014). Hype Cycle. *Gartner*. Retrieved from <http://www.gartner.com/technology/research/methodologies/hype-cycle.jsp>.

Gaudin, S. (2010). Facebook location service could kill Foursquare, ignite privacy issues. *Computerworld*. Retrieved from <http://www.computerworld.com/s/article/9180880/Facebook_location_service_could_kill_Foursquare_ignite_privacy_issues>.

Gellman, B., and Soltani, A. (2013). NSA tracking cellphone locations worldwide, Snowden documents show. *The Washington Post*. Retrieved from <http://www.washingtonpost.com/world/national-security/nsa-tracking-cellphone-locations-worldwide-snowden-documents-show/2013/12/04/5492873a-5cf2-11e3-bc56-c6ca9480ifac_story.html>.

Gergen, K. (2002). The challenge of absent presence. In J. Katz and M. Aakhus (eds), *Perpetual Contact: Mobile Communication, Private Talk, Public Performance*. New York: Cambridge University Press, pp. 227–41.

Gillet, J. (2013). Why emerging markets hold the key to smartphone success for Microsoft-Nokia. *Mobile World Live*. Retrieved from <http://www.mobileworldlive.com/why-emerging-markets-hold-the-key-to-smartphone-success-for-microsoft-nokia>.

Glas, R. (2013). Breaking reality: Exploring pervasive cheating in Foursquare. *Transactions of Digital Game Research Association* 1/1. Retrieved from <http://todigra.org/index.php/todigra/article/view/4/3>.

Gleick, J. (2011). *The Information: A History, a Theory, a Flood*. New York: Vintage Books.

Goffman, E. (1959). *The Presentation of Self in Everyday Life* (rev.). New York: Doubleday.

Goggin, G. (2006). *Cell Phone Culture: Mobile Technology in Everyday Life*. New York: Routledge.

Goggin, G. (2009). Adapting the mobile phone: The iPhone and its consumption. *Continuum: Journal of Media & Cultural Studies* 23/2: 231–44.

Goggin, G. (2010). *Global Mobile Media*. New York: Routledge.

Goggin, G. (2011). Ubiquitous applications: Politics of openness in global mobile cultures. *Digital Creativity* 22/3: 148–59.

Goggin, G. (2012). Google phone rising: The Android and the politics of open source. *Continuum* 26/5: 741–52.

Good, K. D. (2013). From scrapbook to Facebook: A history of personal media assemblage and archives. *New Media & Society* 15/4: 557–73.

Google. (2013a). Android open source project. *Google*. Retrieved from <http://source.android.com/faqs.html#frequently-asked-questions>.

Google. (2013b). Google Play developer policies. *Google*. Retrieved from <http://play.google.com/about/developer-content-policy.html>.

Google. (2013c). What usage limits apply to the Maps API? *Google Maps API*. Retrieved from <https://developers.google.com/maps/faq?csw=1#usagelimits>.

Google. (2014). Our mobile planet. *Google Mobile World Project*. Retrieved from <http://think.withgoogle.com/mobileplanet/en/downloads/>.

Gordon, E., and de Souza e Silva, A. (2011). *Network Locality: How Digital Networks Create a Culture of Location*. Boston, MA: Blackwell.

Green, N. (2002). On the move: Technology, mobility, and the mediation of social time and space. *The Information Society* 18: 281–92.

Greenfield, A. (2006). *Everyware: The Dawning Age of Ubiquitous Computing*. London: New Riders.

Greenwald, G. (2013). NSA collecting phone records of millions of Verizon customers daily. *Guardian*. Retrieved from <http://www.theguardian.com/world/2013/jun/06/nsa-phone-records-verizon-court-order>.

Grindr | learn more. (2014). *Grindr*. Retrieved from <http://grindr.com/learn-more>.

Grundberg, S., Gryta, T., and Connors, W. (2014). Smartphone makers aim at emerging markets with low-end devices. *The Wall Street Journal*. Retrieved from <http://online.wsj.com/news/articles/SB10001424052702304834704579405081452450174>.

Guglielmo, C. (2013). Apple's supplier labor practices in China scrutinized after Foxconn, Pegatron reviews. *Forbes*. Retrieved from <http://www.forbes.com/sites/connieguglielmo/2013/12/12/apples-labor-practices-in-china-scrutinized-after-foxconn-pegatron-reviewed/>.

Ha, A. (2014). CEO Sean Rad says dating app Tinder has made 1 billion matches. *TechCrunch*. Retrieved from <http://techcrunch.com/2014/03/13/tinder-1-billion-matches/>.

Habuchi, I. (2005). Accelerating reflexivity. In Mizuko Ito, D. Okabe, and M. Matsuda (eds), *Personal, Portable, Pedestrian: Mobile Phones in Japanese Life*. Cambridge, MA: MIT Press, pp. 165–82.

Hale, C. (2010). Improving the quality of borders in Google Earth and

Maps. *Google Maps*. Retrieved from <http://google-latlong.blogspot. com/2010/07/improving-quality-of-borders-in-google.html>.

Hall, B. S. (2013). Smartphones have bridged the digital divide. *ReadWrite*. Retrieved from <http://readwrite.com/2013/05/17/smartphones-have-bridged-the-digital-divide>.

Halliday, J. (2010). People worry about over-sharing location from mobiles, study finds. *Guardian*. Retrieved from <http://www.theguardian.com/technology/blog/2010/jul/12/geolocation-foursquare-gowalla-privacy-concerns>.

Hand, M. (2012). *Ubiquitous Photography*. Cambridge: Polity.

Hannam, K., Sheller, M., and Urry, J. (2006). Mobilities, immobilities and moorings. *Mobilities* 1/1: 1–22.

Hardey, M. (2007). The city in the age of Web 2.0: A new synergistic relationship between place and people. *Information Communication and Society* 10/6: 867.

Harrison, S., and Dourish, P. (1996). Re-place-ing space: The roles of place and space in collaborative systems. In *Proceedings of the 1996 ACM Conference on Computer Supported Cooperative Work*. Boston, MA: ACM, pp. 67–76.

Harvey, D. (1991). *The Condition of Postmodernity*. Malden, MA: Blackwell.

Hayles, N. K. (1999). *How We Became Posthuman: Virtual Bodies in Cybernetics, Literature, and Informatics*. Chicago, IL: University of Chicago Press.

Heggestuen, J. (2013). One in every 5 people in the world own a smartphone, one in every 17 own a tablet. *Business Insider*. Retrieved from <http://www.businessinsider.com/smartphone-and-tablet-penetration-2013-10#ixzz2wWOW3PU3>.

Hestres, L. E. (2013). App neutrality: Apple's app store and freedom of expression online. *International Journal of Communication* 7. Retrieved from <http://ijoc.org/index.php/ijoc/article/view/1904>.

Hjorth, L. (2005). Odours of mobility: Mobile phones and Japanese cute culture in the Asia-Pacific. *Journal of Intercultural Studies* 26/1–2: 39–55.

Hjorth, L. (2011). Mobile@game cultures: The place of urban mobile gaming. *Convergence: The International Journal of Research into New Media Technologies* 17/4: 357–71.

Hjorth, L., and Pink, S. (2014). New visualities and the digital wayfarer: Reconceptualizing camera phone photography and locative media. *Mobile Media & Communication* 2/1: 40–57.

Hjorth, L., Wilken, R., and Gu, K. (2012). Ambient intimacy: A case study of the iPhone, presence, and location-based social media in Shanghai, China. In L. Hjorth, J. Burgess, and I. Richardson (eds), *Studying Mobile

Media: Cultural Technologies, Mobile Communication, and the iPhone. New York: Routledge, pp. 43–62.

Hochman, N., and Manovich, L. (2013). Zooming into an Instagram City: Reading the local through social media. *First Monday*, 18(7). Retrieved from <http://journals.uic.edu/ojs/index.php/fm/article/view/4711>.

Hoflich, J. R. (2005). The mobile phone and the dynamic between private and public communication: Results of an international exploratory study. In P. Glotz, S. Bertschi, and C. Locke (eds), *Thumb Culture: The Meaning of Mobile Phones for Society*. London: Transaction Publishers, pp. 123–37.

Hogan, B. (2010). The presentation of self in the age of social media: Distinguishing performances and exhibitions online. *Bulletin of Science, Technology & Society* 30/6: 377–86.

Hoskins, A. (2009). Digital network memory. In A. Erll and A. Rigney (eds), *Mediation, Remediation, and the Dynamics of Cultural Memory*. Berlin: de Gruyter, pp. 91–106.

Howell, E. (2013). Navstar: GPS satellite network. *Space.com*. Retrieved from <http://www.space.com/19794-navstar.html>.

Humphreys, L. (2005). Cellphones in public: Social interactions in a wireless era. *New Media & Society* 7/6: 810–33.

Humphreys, L. (2007). Mobile social networks and social practice: A case study of Dodgeball. *Journal of Computer-Mediated Communication* 13: 341–60.

Humphreys, L. (2010). Mobile social networks and urban public space. *New Media & Society* 12: 763–78.

Humphreys, L. (2012). Connecting, coordinating, cataloguing: Communicative practices on mobile social networks. *Journal of Broadcasting & Electronic Media* 56/4: 494–510.

Humphreys, L., and Liao, T. (2011). Mobile geotagging: Reexamining our interactions with Urban Space. *Journal of Computer-Mediated Communication* 16: 407–23.

IDC. (2013). Android pushes past 80% market share. *International Data Corporation*. Retrieved from <http://www.idc.com/getdoc.jsp?containerId=prUS24442013>.

Ingram, M. (2013). Foursquare closes $41M debt financing, ups the ante on a high-risk gamble to own local recommendations. *Gigaom*. Retrieved from <http://gigaom.com/2013/04/11/foursquare-closes-41m-debt-financing-ups-the-ante-on-a-high-risk-gamble-to-own-local-recommendations/>.

Isaac, M. (2011). Carriers crack down on wireless-tethering app for Android. *Wired*. Retrieved from <http://www.wired.com/gadgetlab/2011/05/wireless-tethering-crackdown/>.

Isaacson, W. (2013). *Steve Jobs*. New York: Simon & Schuster.

Ishikawa, T., Fujiwara, H., Imai, O., and Okabe, A. (2008). Wayfinding with a GPS-based mobile navigation system: A comparison with maps and direct experience. *Journal of Environmental Psychology* 28/1: 74–82.

Ito, M., Okabe, D., and Matsuda, M. (2005). *Personal, Portable, Pedestrian: Mobile Phones in Japanese Life*. Cambridge, MA: MIT Press.

ITU. (2008). Invitation for submission of proposals for candidate radio interface technologies for the terrestrial components of the radio interface(s) for IMT-Advanced and invitation to participate in their subsequent evaluation. *International Telecommunication Union*. Retrieved from <http://wirelessman.org/liaison/docs/L80216-08_008.pdf>.

ITU. (2010). Focus on international regulations for spectrum management and satellite orbits. *International Telecommunication Union*. Retrieved from <http://www.itu.int/net/pressoffice/press_releases/2010/48.aspx#.UqtNydJDtww>.

ITU. (2011). All about the technology. *International Telecommunication Union*. Retrieved from <http://www.itu.int/osg/spu/ni/3G/technology/index.html#Cellular Standards for the Third Generation>.

ITU. (2013). *The World in 2013: ICTs in Facts and Figures*. ITU. Retrieved from <http://www.itu.int/en/ITU-D/Statistics/Documents/facts/ICTFactsFigures2013.pdf>.

ITU. (2014). Statistics. *ITU*. Retrieved from <http://www.itu.int/en/ITU-D/Statistics/Pages/stat/default.aspx>.

Jacobs, F. (2012). The first Google Maps war. *NY Times | Opinionator*. Retrieved from <http://opinionator.blogs.nytimes.com/2012/02/28/the-first-google-maps-war/>.

Jacobs, J. (1961). *The Death and Life of Great American Cities*. New York: Random House.

James, J. (2009). Leapfrogging in mobile telephony: A measure for comparing country performance. *Technological Forecasting and Social Change* 76/7: 991–8.

Jansson, A., and Falkheimer, J. (2006). *Geographies of Communication: The Spatial Turn in Media Studies*. Goteborg, Sweden: Nordicom.

Jenkins, H., Ford, S., and Green, J. (2013). *Spreadable Media: Creating Value and Meaning in a Networked Culture*. New York: New York University Press.

Jensen, O. (2009). Flows of meaning, cultures of movements – urban mobility as meaningful everyday life practice. *Mobilities* 4/1: 139–58.

Kaptelinin, V., and Nardi, B. A. (2006). *Acting with Technology: Activity Theory and Interaction Design*. Cambridge, MA: MIT Press.

Kaptelinin, V., Nardi, B. A., and MacCaulay, C. (1999). The Activity Checklist: A tool for representing the "space" of context. *Interactions* 6/4: 27–39.

Kellerman, A. (2006). *Personal Mobilities*. London: Routledge.

Kelly, K. (2005). *How Technology Evolves*. Presented at the Ted Talks. Retrieved from <http://www.ted.com/talks/kevin_kelly_on_how_tech nology_evolves.html>.

Keyes, A. (2012). This app was made for walking – but is it racist? *NPR.org.* Retrieved from <http://www.npr.org/2012/01/25/145337346/this-app-was-made-for-walking-but-is-it-racist>.

Kincaid, J. (2009). SXSW: Foursquare scores despite its flaws. *TechCrunch*. Retrieved from <http://techcrunch.com/2009/03/18/sxsw-foursquare-scores-despite-its-flaws/>.

Kitchin, R., and Dodge, M. (2011). *Code/Space: Software and Everyday Life*. Cambridge, MA: MIT Press.

Kolmel, B., and Alexakis, S. (2002). Location-based advertising. In *First International Conference on Mobile Business*. Athens, Greece: M-business.

Kraut, R., Kiesler, S., Boneva, B., Cummings, J., Helgeson, V., and Crawford, A. (2002). Internet paradox revisited. *Journal of Social Issues* 58/1: 49–74.

Kraut, R., Patterson, M., Lundmark, V., Kiesler, S., Mukophadhyay, T., and Scherlis, W. (1998). Internet paradox: A social technology that reduces social involvement and psychological well-being? *American Psychologist* 53/9: 1017–31.

Lacy, S. (2011). Foursquare closes $50m at a $600m valuation. *TechCrunch*. Retrieved from <http://techcrunch.com/2011/06/24/foursquare-closes-50m-at-a-600m-valuation/>.

Latour, B. (1987). *Science in Action: How to Follow Scientists and Engineers through Society*. Cambridge, MA: Harvard University Press.

Latour, B. (2005). *Reassembling the Social: An Introduction to Actor-Network Theory*. Oxford: Oxford University Press.

Lederer, S., Mankoff, J., and Dey, A. K. (2003). Who wants to know what when? Privacy preference determinants in ubiquitous computing. In *CHI '03 Extended Abstracts on Human Factors in Computing Systems*. New York: ACM, pp. 724–5.

Lee, T. B. (2013). Of course Snapchat could be worth $3 billion. *Washington Post*. Retrieved from <http://www.washingtonpost.com/blogs/the-switch/wp/2013/11/13/of-course-snapchat-could-be-worth-3-billion/>.

Lefebvre, H. (1991). *The Production of Space*. Malden, MA: Blackwell.

Lehtonen, T., and Mänpää, P. (1997). Shopping in the East Centre Mall. In P. Falk and C. Campbell (eds), *The Shopping Experience*. London: Sage, pp. 136–65.

Licoppe, C. (2004). Connected presence: The emergence of a new repertoire for managing social relationships in a changing communication technoscape. *Environment and Planning D: Society and Space* 22: 135–56.

Licoppe, C. (in press). Living inside location-aware mobile social information: The pragmatics of Foursquare notifications. In J. Katz (ed.), *Living Inside Mobile Information*. Ohio: Greyden Press

Licoppe, C., and Inada, Y. (2009). Mediated co-proximity and its dangers in a location-aware community: A case of stalking. In A. de Souza e Silva and D. M. Sutko (eds), *Digital Cityscapes: Merging Digital and Urban Playspaces*. New York: Peter Lang, pp. 100–28.

Lindqvist, J., Cranshaw, J., Wiese, J., Hong, J., and Zimmerman, J. (2011). *I'm the Mayor of My House: Examining Why People Use Foursquare – A Social-Driven Location Sharing Application*. ACM 8/11/05. Vancouver, BC, Canada: ACM.

Ling, R. (2004). *The Mobile Connection: The Cell Phone's Impact on Society*. San Francisco, CA: Morgan Kaufman.

Ling, R., and Donner, J. (2008). *Mobile Phones and Mobile Communication*. Cambridge: Polity.

Luca, M. (2011). Reviews, reputation, and revenue: The case of Yelp.com. *Harvard Business School*. Retrieved from <http://www.hbs.edu/faculty/Publication%20Files/12-016.pdf>.

Lyons, G., and Urry, J. (2005). Travel time use in the information age. *Transportation Research Part A* 39: 257–76.

MacCannell, D. (1999). *The Tourist: A New Theory of the Leisure Class* (2nd edn). Berkeley, CA: University of California Press.

McCullough, M. (2008). Epigraphy and the public library. In A. Aurigi and F. di Cindio (eds), *Augmented Urban Spaces: Articulating the Physical and Electronic City*. Burlington, VT: Ashgate Publishing, pp. 61–72.

McDermott, J. (2013). Foursquare planning to offer check-in data to target ads on other platforms. *AdAge*. Retrieved from <http://adage.com/article/digital/foursquare-start-offering-data-party-advertisers/240843/>.

McClellan, S. (2013). The most popular app in the world is (envelope, please)....Google Maps! *MediaPost*. Retrieved from <http://www.mediapost.com/publications/article/207921/#axzz2jDS7kMYb>.

McPherson, M., Smith-Lovin, L., and Cook, J. M. (2001). Birds of a feather: Homophily in social networks. *Annual Review of Sociology* 27: 415–44.

Maneesoonthorn, C., and Fortin, D. (2006). Texting behaviour and attitudes toward permission mobile advertising: An empirical study of mobile users' acceptance of SMS for marketing purposes. *International Journal of Mobile Marketing* 1/1: 66–72.

Manguel, A. (1997). *A History of Reading*. New York: Penguin Books.

Manovich, L. (2006). The poetics of augmented space. *Visual Communication* 5/2: 219–42.

Marvin, C. (1988). *When Old Technologies Were New: Thinking about Electric Communication in the Late Nineteenth Ccentury*. Oxford: Oxford University Press.

Marwick, A. (2013). *Status Update: Celebrity, Publicity, and Branding in the Social Media Age*. New York: Yale University Press.

Marwick, A., and boyd, d. (2010). I tweet honestly, I tweet passionately: Twitter users, context collapse, and the imagined audience. *New Media & Society* 13/1: 114–33.

Massey, D. (1994). *Place, Space, and Gender*. Minneapolis, MN: University of Minnesota Press.

Massey, D. (2005). *For Space*. London: Sage.

Mayer, C. (2013). The perils of posting scathing reviews on Yelp and Angie's List. *Forbes*. Retrieved from <http://www.forbes.com/sites/nextavenue/2013/01/07/the-perils-of-posting-scathing-reviews-on-yelp-and-angies-list/>.

Mayer-Schönberger, V., and Cukier, K. (2013). *Big Data: A Revolution That Will Transform How We Live, Work, and Think*. New York: Eamon Dolan/ Houghton Mifflin Harcourt.

Merleau-Ponty, M. (1962). *Phenomenology of Perception*. New York: Humanities Press.

Merriman, P. (2004). Driving places: Marc Augé, Non-Places, and the geographies of England's M1 Motorway. *Theory, Culture & Society* 21/4–5: 145–67.

Meyrowitz, J. (1985). *No Sense of Place: The Impact of Electronic Media on Social Behavior*. New York: Oxford University Press.

Miller, C. C., and O'Brien, K. J. (2013). Germany's complicated relationship with Google Street View. *NY Times Bits Blog*. Retrieved from <http://bits.blogs.nytimes.com/2013/04/23/germanys-complicated-relationship-with-google-street-view/>.

Miller, C. R., and Shepherd, D. (2004). Blogging as social action: A genre analysis of the weblog. In L. Gurak, S. Antonijevic, L. Johnson, C. Ratliff, and J. Reyman (eds), *Into the Blogosphere: Rhetoric, Community, and Culture of Weblogs*. Minneapolis, MN: University of Minnesota; available at <http://blog.lib.umn.edu/blogosphere/blogging_as_social_action.html>.

Monmonier, M. S. (2002). *Spying with Maps: Surveillance Technologies and the Future of Privacy*. Chicago, IL: University of Chicago Press.

Monson, K. (2009). Foursquare is the new Twitter at SXSW. *PCMag*. Retrieved from <http://appscout.pcmag.com/social-networking/273355-foursquare-is-the-new-twitter-at-sxsw>.

Montello, D. R., and Freundschuh, S. (2005). Cognition of geographic information. In R. B. McMaster and E. B. Usery (eds), *A Research Agenda for Geographic Information Science*. Boca Raton, FL: CRC Press, pp. 61–91.

Montgomery, J. (1998). Making a city: Urbanity, vitality, and urban design. *Journal of Urban Design* 3/1: 93–116.

Moore, J. (2011). Building a recommendation engine, Foursquare style. *Foursquare Blog*. Retrieved from <http://engineering.foursquare.com/2011/03/22/building-a-recommendation-engine-foursquare-style/>.

Moravec, H. (1990). *Mind Children: The Future of Robot and Human Intelligence*. Cambridge, MA: Harvard University Press.

Morawczynski, O. (2009). Examining the usage and impact of transformational m-banking in Kenya. In *Internationalization, Design and Global Development* (vol. 5623). Berlin and Heidelberg: Springer, pp. 495–504.

Morgan, K. (2004). The exaggerated death of geography: Learning, proximity, and territorial systems. *Journal of Economic Geography* 4: 3–21.

Moth, D. (2012). Nielsen finds 33% of U.S. mobile users deem location-based ads useful. *Econsultancy*. Retrieved from <http://econsultancy.com/blog/9282-nielsen-finds-33-of-us-mobile-users-deem-location-based-ads-useful?utm_campaign=bloglikes&utm_medium=social network&utm_source=facebook>.

Mozur, P., and Luk, L. (2013). China issues 4G mobile licenses. *The Wall Street Journal*. Retrieved from <http://online.wsj.com/news/articles/SB10001424052702303722104579237573313786190>.

Münzer, S., Zimmer, H. D., Schwalm, M., Baus, J., and Aslan, I. (2006). Computer-assisted navigation and the acquisition of route and survey knowledge. *Journal of Environmental Psychology* 26/4: 300–8.

Murphy, H. (2014). Ominous text message sent to protesters in Kiev sends chills around the internet. *New York Times-The Lede*. Retrieved from <http://thelede.blogs.nytimes.com/2014/01/22/ominous-text-message-sent-to-protesters-in-kiev-sends-chills-around-the-internet/>.

Musil, S. (2013). SK Telecom launches world's first LTE-Advanced network. *CNET*. Retrieved from <http://news.cnet.com/8301-1035_3-57591040-94/sk-telecom-launches-worlds-first-lte-advanced-network/>.

mWomen. (2012). *Striving and Surviving: Exploring the Lives of Women at the Base of the Pyramid*. GSMA mWomen. Retrieved from <http://www.gsma.com/mobilefordevelopment/wp-content/uploads/2013/01/GSMA_mWomen_Striving_and_Surviving-Exploring_the_Lives_of_BOP_Women.pdf>.

Negroponte, N. (1995). *Being Digital*. New York: Vintage Books.

Nielsen, P., and Fjuk, A. (2010). The reality beyond the hype: Mobile Internet is primarily an extension of PC-based Internet. *The Information Society* 26/5: 375–82.

No more there. (1994). *Youtube*. Retrieved from <http://www.youtube. com/watch?v=nJhRPBJPoOo&feature=youtube_gdata_player>.

Oakes, C. (1998). "E911" turns cell phones into tracking devices. *Wired*. Retrieved from <http://www.wired.com/science/discoveries/ news/1998/01/9502>.

Ofcom. (2013). Communications market report 2013. *Ofcom*. Retrieved from <http://stakeholders.ofcom.org.uk/binaries/research/cmr/cmr13 /2013_U.K._CMR.pdf>.

Olson, P. (2014). Why Google's Waze is trading user data with local governments. *Forbes*. Retrieved from <http://www.forbes.com/sites/par myolson/2014/07/07/why-google-waze-helps-local-governments-track-its-users/>.

Ozkul, D., and Gauntlett, D. (2013). Locative media in the city: Drawing maps and telling stories. In J. Farman (ed.), *The Mobile Story: Narrative Practices with Locative Technologies*. New York: Routledge, pp. 113–28.

P.L. (2014). Devices and desires. *The Economist*. Retrieved from <http:// www.economist.com/blogs/schumpeter/2014/02/mobile-world-con gress>.

Page, X., and Kobsa, A. (2009). The circles of Latitude: Adoption and usage of location tracking in online social networking (vol. 4). Presented at the IEEE International Conference on Computational Science and Engineering, 2009. CSE '09, pp. 1027–30.

Panzarino, M. (2014). Foursquare gets $15m and licensing deal from Microsoft to power location context for Windows and mobile. *TechCrunch*. Retrieved from <http://techcrunch.com/2014/02/04/four square-cuts-15m-deal-with-microsoft-to-power-location-and-context-for-windows-and-mobile/>.

Pariser, E. (2011). *The Filter Bubble: What the Internet is Hiding from You*. New York: Penguin Books.

Parks, L. (2005). *Cultures in Orbit: Satellites and the Televisual*. New York: Duke University Press.

Parr, P. (2010). Dear Foursquare: This is not the right time to sell. *Mashable*. Retrieved from <http://mashable.com/2010/04/17/dear-foursquare/>.

Peters, J. D. (1999). *Speaking into the Air: A History of the Idea of Communication*. Chicago, IL: University of Chicago Press.

Pickering, A. (2010). *The Cybernetic Brain*. Chicago, IL: University of Chicago Press.

Pickles, J. (2004). *A History of Spaces: Cartographic Reason, Mapping, and the Geo-coded World*. New York: Routledge.

Pilkington, E., and Johnson, B. (2007). iPhone causes big Apple swarm in Big Apple storms. *Guardian*. Retrieved from <http://www.theguardian. com/news/2007/jun/29/usnews.apple>.

Pinch, T. J., and Bijker, W. E. (1987). The social construction of facts and artifacts: Or how the sociology of science and the sociology of technology might benefit each other. In W. E. Bijker, T. P. Hughes, and T. J. Pinch (eds), *The Social Construction of Technological Systems: New Directions in the Sociology and History of Technology*. Cambridge, MA: MIT Press, pp. 17–50.

Pollack, N. (2010). Behind Foursquare and Gowalla: The great check-in battle. *Wired U.K.* Retrieved from <http://www.wired.co.uk/maga zine/archive/2010/07/features/behind-foursquare-and-gowalla-the-gr eat-check-in-battle>.

Popkin, H. (2013). Three quarters of smartphone users use location services, says study. *NBC News*. Retrieved from <http://www.nbcnews. com/technology/three-quarters-smartphone-users-share-their-location-says-study-8C11139750>.

Privco's Top 10 2013 Predictions. (2013). *Privco*. Retrieved from <http:// www.privco.com/privcos-2013-private-company-predictions-6-10>.

Quenida, D. (2013). Cellphones as a modern irritant. *New York Times*. Retrieved from <http://well.blogs.nytimes.com/2013/03/13/study-adds-to-evidence-of-cellphone-distraction/>.

Quiroz, P. A. (2013). From finding the perfect love online to satellite dating and "loving-the-one-you're near": A look at Grindr, Skout, Plenty of Fish, Meet Moi, Zoosk and assisted serendipity. *Humanity & Society* 37/2: 181–5.

Raice, S., and Ante, S. E. (2013). Insta-Rich: $1 billion for Instagram. *The Wall Street Journal*. Retrieved from <http://online.wsj.com/news/arti cles/ SB10001424052702303815404577333840377381670>.

Rainie, L., and Wellman, B. (2012). *Networked: The New Social Operating System*. Cambridge, MA: MIT Press.

Raynes-Goldie, K. (2010). Aliases, creeping, and wall cleaning: Understanding privacy in the age of Facebook. *First Monday* 15/1. Retrieved from <http://firstmonday.org/ojs/index.php/fm/article/ view/2775/2432>.

Reisinger, D. (2013). AT&T's 4G LTE wins award for "fastest mobile network." *CNET*. Retrieved from <http://news.cnet.com/8301-1035_3-57589606-94/at-ts-4g-lte-wins-award-for-fastest-mobile-network/>.

Relph, E. (1976). *Place and Placelessness*. London: Pion.

Rheingold, H. (2002). *Smart Mobs: The Next Social Revolution*. Cambridge, MA: Perseus Publishing.

Ribeiro, J. (2009). Google placates India, China with different map versions. *PCWorld*. Retrieved from <http://www.pcworld.com/arti cle/174205/article.html>.

Rider Spoke. (2013). *Blast Theory*. Retrieved from <http://www.blastthe ory.co.uk/projects/rider-spoke/>.

Rip, M. R., and Hasik, J. M. (2002). *The Precision Revolution: GPS and the Future of Aerial Warfare.* Annapolis, MD: Naval Institute Press.

Rosen, R. J. (2012). "Time and space has been completely annihilated." *The Atlantic.* Retrieved from <http://www.theatlantic.com/technology/archive/2012/02/time-and-space-has-been-completely-annihilated/253103/>.

Rovio privacy policy. (2013). *Rovio.* Retrieved from <http://www.rovio.com/privacy>.

Rowinski, D. (2014). How we are entering the second phase of the mobile revolution. *ReadWrite.* Retrieved from <http://readwrite.com/2014/01/10/mobile-everywhere-smart-devices-internet-things>.

Sager, I. (2012). Before iPhone and Android came Simon, the first smartphone. *BusinessWeek: technology.* Retrieved from <http://www.businessweek.com/articles/2012-06-29/before-iphone-and-android-came-simon-the-first-smartphone#p2>.

Savage, C. (2013). In test project, NSA tracked cellphone locations. *The New York Times.* Retrieved from <http://www.nytimes.com/2013/10/03/us/nsa-experiment-traced-us-cellphone-locations.html>.

Schivelbusch, W. (1986). *The Railway Journey: The Industrialization of Time and Space in the 19th Century.* Berkeley and Los Angeles, CA: University of California Press.

Schmiedl, G., Siedl, M., and Temper, K. (2009). Mobile phone web browsing – A study on usage and usability of the mobile web. Presented at the MobileHCI'09, Bonn, Germany.

Schwartz, R., and Halegoua, G. (in press). The spatial self: Location-based identity performance on social media. *New Media & Society.*

Sennett, R. (1977). *The Fall of Public Man.* New York: Knopf.

Sheller, M. (2010). Air mobilities on the U.S.–Caribbean border: Open skies and closed gates. *The Communication Review* 13/4: 269–88.

Sheller, M., and Urry, J. (2006). The new mobilities paradigm. *Environment and Planning A* 38/2: 207–26.

Shklovski, I., Vertesi, J., Troshynski, E., and Dourish, P. (2009). The commodification of location: Dynamics of power in location-based systems. In *Proceedings of the 11th International Conference on Ubiquitous Computing.* New York: ACM, pp. 11–20.

Siegler, M. G. (2009). Confirmed: Foursquare gets $1.35 million to play with from Union Square and O'Reilly AlphaTech. *TechCrunch.* Retrieved from <http://techcrunch.com/2009/09/04/confirmed-foursquare-gets-135-million-to-play-with/>.

Siegler, M. G. (2010). Android is as open as the clenched fist I'd like to punch the carriers with. *TechCrunch.* Retrieved from <http://techcrunch.com/2010/09/09/android-open/>.

Simmel, G. (1950). *The Sociology of Georg Simmel*. New York: Free Press.

Smith, A. (2013). *Smartphone Ownership – 2013 Update*. PEW Internet and American Life Project. Retrieved from <http://pewinternet.org/~/media//Files/Reports/2013/PIP_Smartphone_adoption_2013.pdf>.

Soghoian, C. (2013). Federal judge: Only powered-off cell phones deserve privacy protections. *American Civil Liberties Union*. Retrieved from <https://www.aclu.org/blog/technology-and-liberty-national-security/federal-judge-only-powered-cell-phones-deserve-privacy>.

Soja, E. (1996). *Thirdspace: Journeys to Los Angeles and Other Real-and-Imagined Places*. Malden, MA: Blackwell Publishers.

Solove, D. (2004). *The Digital Person: Technology and Privacy in the Information Age*. New York: New York University Press.

Solove, D. (2008). *Understanding Privacy*. Cambridge, MA: Harvard University Press.

Solove, D. (2011). Why privacy matters even if you have "nothing to hide." *The Chronicle of Higher Education*. Retrieved from <http://chronicle.com/article/Why-Privacy-Matters-Even-if/127461/>.

Song, V. (2010). Meet Chris Tindal, the new "mayor" at City Hall. *The Toronto Star*. Retrieved from <http://www.thestar.com/life/2010/03/05/theres_a_new_mayor_in_town.html>.

Sontag, S. (2001). *On Photography*. New York: Picador.

Sparrow, B., Liu, J., and Wegner, D. M. (2011). Google effects on memory: Cognitive consequences of having information at our fingertips. *Science* 333/6043: 776–8.

Steinmueller, W. E. (2001). ICTs and the possibilities for leapfrogging by developing countries. *International Labour Review* 140/2: 193–210.

Sutko, D. M., and de Souza e Silva, A. (2011). Location-aware mobile media and urban sociability. *New Media & Society* 13/5: 807–23.

Sweeney, P. J. (2012). Is Foursquare's bubble about to burst? *Forbes*. Retrieved from <http://www.forbes.com/sites/ciocentral/2012/11/23/is-foursquares-bubble-about-to-burst/>.

Swisher, K. (2013). Exclusive: Foursquare raises a $35 million round and adds DFJ's Schuler to the board. *AllThingsD*. Retrieved from <http://allthingsd.com/20131219/exclusive-foursquare-raises-35-million-round-and-adds-dfjs-schuler-to-the-board/>.

Talbot, D. (2013). Big data from cheap phones. *MIT Technology Review*. Retrieved from <http://www.technologyreview.com/featured-story/513721/big-data-from-cheap-phones/>.

Tang, K. P., Lin, J., Hong, J. I., Siewiorek, D. P., and Sadeh, N. (2010). Rethinking location sharing: Exploring the implications of social-driven vs. purpose-driven location sharing. In *Proceedings of the 12th ACM International Conference on Ubiquitous Computing*. New York: ACM, pp. 85–94.

Taylor, C. (2012a). Dennis Crowley on reinventing Foursquare: De-emphasizing check-ins, digging into data, moving toward revenue. *TechCrunch*. Retrieved from <http://techcrunch.com/2012/06/07/dennis-crowley-on-foursquare-5-update-video/>.

Taylor, C. (2012b). Yelp closes 5-star IPO day with $1.47 billion valuation. *TechCrunch*. Retrieved from <http://techcrunch.com/2012/03/02/yelp-closes-5-star-ipo-day-with-1-47-billion-valuation/>.

TechCrunch. (2014). Tinder wins best new startup of 2013. *TechCrunch*. Retrieved from <http://techcrunch.com/video/tinder-wins-best-new-startup-of-2013-crunchies-awards-2013/518118930/>.

Thomas, O. (2012). Instagram's financial report: No revenues, $2.7 million in losses, $5 million in the bank. *Business Insider*. Retrieved from <http://www.businessinsider.com/instagram-finances-2012-8>.

Thurm, S., and Kane, Y. I. (2010). Your applications are watching you. *The Wall Street Journal*. Retrieved from <http://online.wsj.com/article/SB10001424052748704694004576020083703574602.html?mod=WSJ_hp_LEFTTopStories>.

Tuan, Y. (1977). *Space and Place: The Perspective of Experience*. Minneapolis, MN: University of Minnesota Press.

Turkle, S. (2010). *Alone Together: Why We Expect More from Technology and Less from Each Other*. New York: Basic Books.

Turow, J. (2012). *The Daily You: How the New Advertising Industry is Defining Your Identity and Your Worth*. New York: Yale University Press.

Unni, R., and Harmon, R. (2007). Perceived effectiveness of push vs pull mobile location-based advertising. *Journal of Interactive Advertising* 7/2. Retrieved from <http://jiad.org/article91.html

Urban Tapestries. (2005). *Social Matrices*. Retrieved from http://research.urbantapestries.net/>.

Urry, J. (2007). *Mobilities*. Cambridge: Polity.

Vaidhyanathan, S. (2011). *The Googlization of Everything (and Why We Should Worry)*. Berkeley and Los Angeles, CA: University of California Press.

Van Grove, J. (2009). Foursquare is the breakout mobile app at SXSW. *Mashable*. Retrieved from <http://mashable.com/2009/03/16/foursquare/>.

Vazquez, P. M. (2011). American Express partners with Foursquare at SXSW. *The Future of Retail/ A PSFK Report*. Retrieved from <http://www.psfk.com/2011/03/american-express-partners-with-foursquare-at-sxsw.html>.

Versace, C. (2013). Mapping heats up as Apple buys Embark, Google integrates Waze ... what's next? *Forbes*. Retrieved from <http://www.forbes.

com/sites/chrisversace/2013/08/26/mapping-heats-up-as-apple-buys-embark-google-integrates-waze-whats-next/>.

Virilio, P. (1997). *Open Sky*. London and New York: Verso.

Warner, J. (2005). Business shouldn't be moaning about the climate change agenda, but embracing it. *The Independent*. Retrieved from <http://www.independent.co.uk/news/business/comment/jeremy-warners-out look-business-shouldnt-be-moaning-about-the-climate-change-agenda-but-embracing-it-509786.html>.

Waters, W., and Winter, S. (2011). A wayfinding aid to increase navigator independence. *Journal of Spatial Information Science* 3: 103–22.

Weintraub, J. (1997). The theory and politics of the public/private distinction. In J. Weintraub and K. Kumar (eds), *Public and Private in Thought and Practice: Perspectives on a Grand Dichotomy*. Chicago, IL: University of Chicago Press, pp. 1–42.

Weintraub, S. (2010). Why Verizon and Skype's backdoor deal hurts Android. *CNNMoney*. Retrieved from <http://tech.fortune.cnn.com/2010/08/21/why-verizon-and-skypes-backdoor-deal-hurts-android/>.

Weiser, M., Gold, R., and Brown, J. S. (1999). The origins of ubiquitous computing research at PARC in the late 1980's. *IBM Systems Journal* 38/4: 693–6.

Wellman, B. (2002). Little boxes, globalization, and networked individualism. In M. Tanabe, P. Van den Besselaar, and T. Ishida (eds), *Digital Cities II: Computational and Sociological Approaches*. Berlin: Springer, pp. 10–26.

Wilhelm, A. (2012). Google's loss, Microsoft's gain, and Apple's passing fancy: Meet OpenStreetMap. *The Next Web*. Retrieved from <http://the nextweb.com/insider/2012/03/27/googles-loss-microsofts-gain-and-ap ples-passing-fancy-meet-openstreetmap/>.

Wilken, R. (2010). A community of strangers? Mobile media, art, tactility and urban encounters with the other. *Mobilities* 5/4: 449–68.

Willis, K. S., Hölscher, C., Wilbertz, G., and Li, C. (2009). A comparison of spatial knowledge acquisition with maps and mobile maps. *Distributed and Mobile Spatial Computing* 33/2: 100–10.

Wilson, J. (2006). 3g to Web 2.0? Can mobile telephony become an architecture of participation? *Convergence: The International Journal of Research into New Media Technologies* 12/2: 229–42.

Wood, D. (1992). *The Power of Maps*. New York: Guilford Press.

Wood, D., and Graham, S. (2005). Permeable boundaries in the software-sorted society: Surveillance and the differentiation of mobility. In M. Sheller and J. Urry (eds), *Mobile Technologies of the City*. London: Routledge, p. 177.

Worstall, T. (2013). Why the reviewer card is such a terrible idea.

Forbes. Retrieved from <http://www.forbes.com/sites/timworstall/2013/01/24/why-the-reviewercard-is-such-a-terrible-idea/>.

Wortham, J. (2009). Foursquare seeks to turn nightlife into a game. *Bits Blog-NY Times.* Retrieved from <http://bits.blogs.nytimes.com/2009/03/13/foursquare-seeks-to-turn-nightlife-into-a-game/>.

Wortham, J. (2011). American Express teams with Foursquare. *The New York Times.* Retrieved from <http://www.nytimes.com/2011/06/23/technology/23locate.html>.

Wroclawski, S. (2014). Why the world needs OpenStreetMap. *Guardian.* Retrieved from <http://www.theguardian.com/technology/2014/jan/14/why-the-world-needs-openstreetmap>.

Yarow, J. (2010). Foursquare will get 1 million users faster than Twitter did. *Business Insider.* Retrieved from <http://www.businessinsider.com/foursquare-will-get-its-1-million-users-faster-than-twitter-did-2010-3>.

Zara, C. (2013). Small businesses fed up with Yelp "extortion." *International Business Times.* Retrieved from <http://www.ibtimes.com/yelp-extortion-rampant-say-small-business-owners-class-action-lawsuit-against-review-bully-appealed>.

Zetter, K. (2009). Feds "pinged" sprint GPS data 8 million times over a year. *Wired.* Retrieved from http://www.wired.com/threatlevel/2009/12/gps-data/

Zickuhr, K. (2013). *Location-based Services.* Washington, DC: PEW Internet and American Life Project. Retrieved from <http://www.pewinternet.org/~/media/Files/Report/2013/PIP_Location-based%20services%202013.pdf>.

Zittrain, J. (2008). *The Future of the Internet – And How To Stop It.* Harrisonburg, VA: Yale University Press.

Index